P9-DBQ-121

Grand Diplôme® Cooking Course

Volume 1

Grand Diplôme® Cooking Course

A Danbury Press Book

The Danbury Press

a division of Grolier Enterprises, Inc.

Robert B. Clarke Publisher

This book has been adapted from the Grand Diplôme Cooking Course, originally published by Purnell Cookery, U.S.A.

Library of Congress Catalog Card Number: 72-13896

Filmsetting by Petty and Sons Ltd., Leeds, England.
Printed in the United States of America

99

All recipes have been tested either at the Cordon Bleu Cookery School in London or in our U.S. test kitchens.

Note: all recipe quantities in this book serve 4 people unless otherwise stated.

From the Publisher

There are thousands of cookbooks. And every day, newspapers and magazines offer hundreds of recipes – good, bad and indifferent. But never before has anyone published a series of books that guides you from the basics of good cooking to the complicated dishes that make a special occasion really special.

This Grand Diplôme Cooking Course is exactly that. As you read each book, you'll quickly become familiar with simple cooking techniques, like pastry-making and homemade soups. Gradually, just as you would at the world-famous Cordon Bleu Cookery School in London, you'll find yourself becoming a better and better cook, sampling a few ethnic dishes along the way, so that in a few months you will have mastered a great deal more than the intricacies of French gâteaux and the secrets of a satin-smooth sauce.

Every volume will include over one hundred varied recipes in our basic lessons and suggested menus, so you can practice in your own home, according to your own budget. There will be ideas for every occasion, from the intimate dinner to a wedding buffet with all the trimmings. And Timetables, so you won't waste any time in the kitchen.

Robert B Clarke

What it's all about...

Never before have you had the chance to learn to cook not just well but superbly – in the manner of the great French chefs – by following a complete cooking course in the comfort of your own home.

We combed the world to find the school with a teaching method that we believed would work best for you when presented in book form as an instructional cooking course. We found it at the Cordon Bleu Cookery School in London, England, whose Principal, Rosemary Hume, not only trained in France at the Cordon Bleu School of Paris under the famous Chef Pellaprat, but whose graduates are sought after by companies and households throughout the world.

Her tried and tested cooking methods have been specially adapted for North America to enable you to share the London School's cooking expertise. Now you can learn in your own time from these carefully planned books, to cook dishes that you've never before attempted and so win compliments and praise from both family and friends.

This full-scale cooking course combines the advantages of expert instruction (meet your teachers on page 9) with the freedom to work in your own home, in your own time. And by purchasing the Grand Diplôme Cooking Course series of books, you will build up a complete reference work for your kitchen library – over 2,000 recipes always handy for family or party meals.

Today the London Cordon Bleu Cookery School's method of cooking is also justly world-renowned. You, too, can learn from it. And since we're sure you would like to know more about the London School, the photographs on pages 10–11 take you behind the scenes during classes and a students' Open Day reception.

Basic techniques

From the very first volume of the Grand Diplôme Cooking Course, you have a choice of four party menus so you will be able to produce a three-course party meal, even if you have never before cooked anything more ambitious than a boiled egg. Here, the secret of success lies very largely with the Grand Diplôme method of including a Timetable, telling you what can be prepared ahead of time – and in what order the various stages should be worked. If you follow these Timetables and work plans, you will be surprised at how much time you learn to save in preparing menus. Of course, you don't have to cook the whole of any one of these meals at once. Choose one dish at a time and experiment to suit your day-to-day needs.

Learn as you go

Each volume covers four or more of the basic cooking techniques, plus essential kitchen skills and specialized dishes. Most cooking schools give single demonstrations for each of these techniques, starting with the simplest method at the beginning and finishing with advanced applications. With the Grand Diplôme Cooking Course, you are not tied to a conventional order of priorities. Each main subject, such as broiling, roasting, sautéing, cake- and pastry-making etc., is treated in depth through one or more books, with detailed instructions and illustrations in color – and with advice on the most suitable cooking equipment to use.

These sections continue with some twenty or more related recipes, simple and advanced, for small budgets and special occasions, so that you can quickly put into practice what you learn from the lessons and general instructions. The text of each basic recipe explains every stage in detail until more advanced techniques are reached. Relevant short cuts and likely danger points – called 'Watchpoints' – are noted, so experienced cooks can also learn something new.

The photographs – all in full color – show what the finished dishes should look like, without too many decorative accessories to disguise the main points. Where necessary, step-by-step photographs are also given, as well as diagrams to illustrate particular methods of cooking, details of carving and so on. Once you have mastered the basic techniques, you will be able to draw on the experience you've gained and go on to try out the exciting recipes from Russia, China, India and Mexico – to name but a few of the specialty cooking sections in store.

A list of your Grand Diplôme Cooking Course subjects covered in these volumes is on the next page.

Your Grand Diplôme Cooking Course Subjects

The Grand Diplôme Cooking Course covers:
Roasting; boiling and steaming; boning, cutting up and carving poultry; pot roasting; frying; broiling; sautéing; casserole cooking; how to make pâtés and terrines; stewing; braising and marinating; preparing and carving meat; slow and spit roasting; preparing and cooking game; advanced entrées; sausages, rechauffées, dealing with variety meats; making galantines and chaudfroids.

Making stock, soup, basic brown, white, butter – and sweet – sauces; cooking with milk, rice, chocolate, nuts, cheese, pasta, dried vegetables and wine.

Cooking with eggs; making omelets, roulades, hot and cold soufflés, waffles, crêpes and pancakes.

Dealing with fruit and vegetables, seasonal salads, side salads; appetizers and hors d'oeuvre; poaching fruit; making savory molds, cleared and uncleared gelatins and aspics; preserving jam, jellies, pickles and relishes; homemade vinegars; and using herbs and spices.

Shellfish; rich fish and white fish – elementary and advanced dishes.

Making pastry – flaky, pie, rough puff and choux; flans, pies, cakes both plain and festive; French and other Continental pâtisseries and gâteaux; English cakes; home-baked bread, biscuits, meringues, sponge cakes, cookies and coffee cakes; petit fours; homemade candies; making sherbet and ice cream, frappés, granités and iced desserts.

Special occasion menus; menu-planning and catering for parties of all sizes, all ages, from a teenage celebration to a Golden Wedding buffet; planning vacation cooking and foreign foods for summer. Russian cooking; Italian cooking; German cooking; English regional dishes; Scandinavian cooking; Jewish cooking; Mexican; Middle Eastern, Japanese and Chinese cooking; the food of Spain and Portugal; Indian and Pakistani dishes, tropical cooking and French haute cuisine.

All recipes have been tested either at the Cordon Bleu Cookery School in London or in our U.S. test kitchens.

Note: all recipe quantities in this book serve 4 people unless otherwise stated.

Meet Your Teachers

The two Principals of the world-famous Cordon Bleu Cookery School in London, England, and the distinguished Cordon Bleu-trained former associate editor of *Gourmet* magazine

ANNE WILLAN

Anne Willan's culinary skills have become well known in three capitals: London, where she studied and taught at the Cordon Bleu Cookery School; Paris, where she earned the coveted 'Grand Diplóme du Cordon Bleu' and, in her spare time, prepared dinner parties for the most exacting gourmet audience in the world; and Washington, D.C., where she was food editor of *The Washington Evening Star* for two years.

Before she introduced *The Star's* many readers to the pleasures of fine cuisine, Anne was an associate editor of the New York-based *Gourmet* magazine. There she became familiar with some of the problems—and the rewards—of adapting European recipes and techniques for a North American audience.

ROSEMARY HUME

Rosemary Hume, a graduate of the Cordon Bleu Cooking School of Paris, carried on their teaching tradition in London in the early 1930's. Her school, first named 'Au Petit Cordon Bleu', was closed during World War II but re-opened in 1945 as the Cordon Bleu Cookery School and has since gone from success to success.

Under her expert eye many of the best cooks around the world have been trained. Capable and dedicated, Rosemary Hume says, 'Cooking should be fun', and her knowledge, talent for teaching and boundless enthusiasm have made it so for every cook she has coaxed, guided and inspired during the last forty years. She was recently awarded a medal, and became a Member of the British Empire in the Birthday Honors List of Queen Elizabeth II.

MURIEL DOWNES

Muriel Downes is the London School's Co-Principal with Rosemary Hume. Once a food specialist in Unilever's experimental kitchens in London and a well-known demonstrator of cooking, Muriel Downes joined the School when it re-opened in 1945. She has always had a great interest in French food and today she travels all over the world, demonstrating and lecturing on the London School's cooking methods and techniques.

'Anyone who really wants to learn good French cooking can—The London Cordon Bleu way,' she insists. Our London School is open to all—schoolgirls, single girls, men of all ages, housewives on big and small budgets—in fact, anyone with the desire to cook well. Follow this Grand Diplóme Cooking Course and you will see what she means.

Inside the London Cordon Bleu Cookery School

1
Rosemary Hume (center), founder and Principal of the Cordon Bleu Cookery School in London, briefs teachers before a class

2
Muriel Downes (right), Co-Principal, gives a demonstration in the lecture hall, with the assistance of a teacher. Here, she is preparing sauté of veal Marengo, and the angled mirror above the work table ensures students see every step

3
Jeannette Kruschandl, Deputy Principal of the London School, puts the finishing touches to a caramel mousse

4,5
At the annual Open Day reception, parents of the students enjoy a magnificent buffet. At front are cold cheese soufflé, couronne of shrimps in aspic (left) and stuffed egg salad; behind these dishes are avocado mousse (left), sole éventail (right) on an oval platter, haddock mousse and tomatoes Gervais. Lastly, there's a salmon mousse and pâtés. And these are only a fraction of the students' full repertoire of recipes

All recipes noted above will be included in the Grand Diplôme Cooking Course books.

3

5

4

From the Editor

Zucchini stuffed with shrimps, leg of lamb with vegetables baked as a savory pot roast, chicken Basquaise cooked in French style with a garnish of onion, ham and green peppers – these are just a few of the tempting dishes that make up the four menus in the first Volume of the Grand Diplôme Cooking Course.

Features begin with the basics of **Roasting Meat**, including descriptions of the best cuts of beef, lamb and pork, and a chart of timing and temperatures. Then come a bevy of traditional accompaniments like Yorkshire pudding for beef, and sage and onion stuffing for pork. Go on to make the perfect **Pie Pastry** melting in a delectable selection of sweet pies, then tackle those indispensable kitchen processes, **Boiling and Steaming**, or try your hand at a sophisticated French standby, the **Omelet.**

Poultry stars in a lesson on the A to Z of choosing, boning, cutting up and carving chicken, duck and goose. Recipes using these techniques include braised duck with olives, chicken Dijonnaise with a piquant mustard sauce, and luxurious chicken Parisienne, boned and stuffed with veal, ham and herbs.

Lastly you can become a skilled **Cake-maker** thanks to the detailed instructions on baking, plus all the recipes that mother made – pound cake, angel cake, devil's food cake – and many more.

At the end of the book are useful reference sections on types of flour used in cooking, basic cooking equipment, measuring and measurements, and oven temperatures and shelf positions. A glossary explains the cooking terms you will come across during the Grand Diplôme Cooking Course. Each Volume of the Course has something for everyone, so have fun in the kitchen. Bon Appétit!

Anne Willan

Contents

All recipes have been tested either at the Cordon Bleu Cookery School in London or in our U.S. test kitchens.

Note: all recipe quantities in this book serve 4 people unless otherwise stated.

COOK AN EASY PARTY DINNER FOR FOUR

Start on a successful 'Grand Diplôme' career with this simple yet elegant dinner menu. With the chicken why not try one of the straightforward white wines known for their crisp, clean taste from the Mâconnais district in southern Burgundy. Or, as a good domestic alternative, for taste and value, choose a California Pinot Blanc, made largely from the same grape. The Timetable on page 16 will guide you through the planning of this first dinner menu in your Grand Diplôme Cooking Course.

Tomatoes Gervais
with Walnut Bread Rolls

Roast Chicken Basquaise
Julienne Potato Cake   *Green Salad*

Mousse au Chocolat
with Cigarettes Russes

White wine – Mâcon Blanc (Côte Mâconnaise)
or Pinot Blanc (California)

An Easy Party Dinner

Chicken Basquaise is garnished with onions, peppers and diced ham. Serve with green salad and julienne potato cake

TIMETABLE

Day before
Make mousse au chocolat, cover and refrigerate; make cigarettes Russes and store in airtight container.
Make vinaigrette dressing.
Make chicken stock (if preparing separately from chicken).

Morning
Peel potatoes; leave whole in cold water. Prepare salad; wrap in paper towels, then in a cloth or plastic bag and refrigerate.
Wrap wholewheat loaf and freeze for 30 minutes.
Prepare chicken for roasting; set in pan, cover with buttered paper and refrigerate until ready to cook.
Scald tomatoes, transfer immediately to cold water but do not peel.
Prepare cream cheese mixture, cover with foil or plastic wrap and refrigerate.
Cut bread and butter slices, add walnuts and complete rolls. Cover with foil, plastic wrap or a damp cloth and refrigerate.

Assemble equipment for final cooking from 6 p.m. for dinner at 8 p.m.

You will find that **cooking times** given in the individual recipes for these dishes have sometimes been adapted in the timetable to help you when cooking and serving them as a party meal.

Order of Work

6:00
Light oven, assemble serving dishes and plates, and put to warm. Cut and dry potatoes; butter pan, fill with potato strips.

6:15
Pour stock around chicken and put in oven. Whip cream and decorate mousses; chill. Peel and fill tomatoes, arrange on platter and chill.

6:35
Baste chicken, turn on side.

6:55
Start cooking potatoes.
Baste and turn chicken onto other side. Prepare and cook chicken Basquaise garnish and reserve.

7:15
Baste chicken and turn breast side up. When cooked, turn oven to low. Deglaze roasting pan, strain and make gravy. Set aside.

7:45
Carve chicken and arrange on platter, cover with foil but do not seal at edges. Keep warm in oven. If potatoes are not cooked, finish cooking on top of stove, then turn out and keep warm. Pour dressing on stuffed tomatoes and put on table.
Reheat garnish, add to chicken and keep warm.

8:00
Serve appetizer. After serving appetizer, spoon a little gravy over the chicken and serve the rest separately; toss salad.

Appetizer

Tomatoes Gervais

4 large, or 8 medium, tomatoes
salt and pepper
2 packages (3 oz each) cream cheese
3–4 tablespoons light cream
2 tablespoons chopped chives
$\frac{1}{2}$ cup vinaigrette dressing (see page 23)
bunch of watercress (for garnish – optional)

Note: if fresh chives are not available, use finely chopped scallions or watercress stalks and add 1 teaspoon thyme, marjoram or basil to the vinaigrette dressing.

The correct cheese to use for this dish is the French 'Petit Suisse' which is available in some specialty stores; however, regular cream cheese is a good substitute.

Method
Peel the tomatoes by placing them in a bowl and covering with boiling water for 10 seconds. Drain and cover them with cold water. The skin can now be removed easily. Cut a slice from the bottom (not stalk end) of each tomato, reserving the slices. Holding the tomato in the hollow of your palm, scoop out the seeds with the handle of a teaspoon, using bowl of spoon to detach the core. (If the spoon is worn and slightly sharp, so much the better.) Drain seeded tomatoes and season the insides lightly with salt. Soften cheese by working it with a wooden spoon through a strainer resting on a bowl, or beat it in an electric mixer. Add enough cream to make a smooth light mixture, season well with salt and pepper and add half the chives.

With a teaspoon, fill tomatoes with cheese mixture, piling it up well, replace slices on a slant, and arrange them on a platter. Spoon over a little of the vinaigrette dressing, reserving some to be added just before serving. Cover and chill for up to 2 hours. Just before serving, garnish with watercress and sprinkle remaining chives over tomatoes. Serve with walnut bread rolls.

Accompaniments to Appetizer

Walnut Bread Rolls

1 lb unsliced whole wheat loaf
4 – 6 tablespoons butter, creamed
$\frac{1}{4}$ cup chopped English walnuts
1–2 teaspoons coarse, or regular salt (preferably freshly ground)

Method
A close-textured loaf of sliced bread can be used for the bread rolls, but thinner, more elegant slices can be cut from an unsliced loaf. (If you freeze the loaf, wrapped, for 30 minutes, this task is much easier.)

Cut the crust from the entire base of the loaf; butter, then slice the loaf lengthwise, i.e. in long slices from one end to the other. Remove the remaining crusts and sprinkle each slice with chopped walnuts and a little salt. Starting from a short end, roll the slice two complete turns, then cut it off, pressing the edge down firmly. Continue until the whole slice is used. Each slice should make 2–3 rolls.

An Easy Party Dinner

A refreshing appetizer, tomatoes Gervais, is garnished with chives and watercress

Roast Chicken Basquaise

$3\frac{1}{2}$–4 lb roasting chicken
salt and pepper
$\frac{1}{4}$ cup butter, softened
3–4 sprigs of fresh tarragon, or 2 teaspoons dried tarragon
2 cups chicken stock
1 teaspoon cornstarch

For garnish
1 green pepper
1 red pepper
2 tablespoons oil
10–12 small onions, peeled
1 cup ($\frac{1}{2}$ lb) lean ham, diced
salt and pepper
1 tablespoon chopped parsley

Method

Wipe inside of chicken with a damp cloth, but do not wash it as this hinders browning and does nothing to improve the flavor. Season the bird inside to penetrate the flesh (seasoning outside does not do this; the salt draws out the juices and prevents browning).

If the bird is not already trussed, do this yourself because a well-trussed chicken keeps its shape better during cooking and is easier to carve when cooked. (Trussing and carving are not difficult when done correctly, as described in the diagrams and instructions on pages 20–21.)

Spread the chicken with half the butter and put the remaining butter inside with the tarragon and seasoning. Place chicken, breast side up, in a roasting pan, with half the chicken stock. Cover loosely with foil or buttered brown paper and roast in a hot oven (400°F) for $1\frac{1}{4}$ hours or until tender.

After the first 20 minutes, when the flesh should be lightly cooked but not browned, baste and turn on one side. Baste and turn again after another 20 minutes. Finish cooking with breast upwards, removing foil or paper for the last few minutes. The chicken should be well browned all over.

To test if chicken is done, take a skewer or a finely pointed knife and pierce the flesh of the thigh. The liquid which runs out should be quite clear; if it is at all pink, continue cooking. A bird which has been frozen usually takes longer to cook and brown as it is so moist.

When cooked, take chicken from the oven, let stand 10–15 minutes in a warm place, then carve it on a wooden board. If the juices in the pan have not cooked down to a glaze (a sticky consistency) simmer on top of the stove over low heat until the juices reduce and become brown and sticky. To make gravy add the remaining cup of stock.

Deglaze pan by scraping it with the basting spoon to dissolve juices, and strain mixture into a small saucepan. To thicken slightly and to blend the butter (used for roasting) into the stock, stir the cornstarch with 1 tablespoon of water until dissolved, then whisk into the stock. Bring to a boil, stirring continuously, until mixture thickens; simmer 2 minutes. The gravy will be clear and needs no further cooking. Adjust seasoning to taste and keep hot.

For garnish, cut the cores from peppers, remove seeds, cut flesh into strips and blanch. Heat the oil in a pan and add the onions; cook over medium heat for 8 minutes, or until lightly brown. Stir in the ham with the sliced peppers, cover and cook for 3–4 minutes over low heat or until peppers are just tender. Add salt and pepper to taste, stir in parsley.

Arrange chicken along one side of a serving dish and pile the garnish on the other. Spoon a little gravy over chicken and serve the rest separately. Accompany the chicken with a julienne potato cake.

Recipes for julienne potato cake and green salad are on page 22.

The **Basque country** lies both in France and Spain, and is divided by the Pyrénées. The people of the region have developed an individual cuisine although much has been borrowed from both cultures. Free use of pimiento (green and red peppers here) suggests Spanish influence; ham is a specialty of Bayonne, the old Basque gastronomic capital'.

Basting

This keeps the bird, or a cut of meat moist and juicy while it is roasting. To baste properly, take the pan from the oven, closing the door, and spoon hot liquid several times over the chicken with a large metal spoon or basting bulb. When basting and turning, never pierce the flesh of the bird with a fork, or it will lose its succulent juices. If possible, turn it with two spoons. If a metal fork is used, be sure it goes inside the bird or into its back and does not pierce the breast, legs or thighs until ready to test at end of cooking.

Chicken Stock

When cooking a whole chicken, make stock from the giblets (neck, gizzard, heart and feet, if available); never add the liver because it gives a bitter flavor. (The liver is better for making pâté or sautéed for a snack.) Heat a thick saucepan with scarcely enough fat to cover the base; then add giblets and an onion, halved and washed but not peeled, and 'dry fry' over a high heat until lightly browned. Remove pan from heat and add 1 quart of cold water. Add $\frac{1}{4}$ teaspoon salt, a few peppercorns, and a bouquet garni (bay leaf, thyme, and parsley). Cover and simmer gently for 1–2 hours. When roasting, you can make stock in the same pan as the chicken by browning the giblets and onion with the chicken as it roasts and then adding 1 cup of water.

An Easy Party Dinner

Tomatoes Gervais, chicken Basquaise and green salad

Trussing a chicken

The best way to truss a chicken is to use string and a special long trussing needle. However, it is quite possible to hold the bird firmly together in the same position by using skewers and tying string around them.

Fold flap of skin over back of neck end, fold ends of wing pinions backwards and under to hold neck skin in position. Place bird on back, press legs down into sides to plump up breast.

To truss with a needle

1 Thread trussing needle with a strong thread or thin string. Insert needle through wing nearest you, then through thigh and body to emerge in same position on far side.

2 Insert needle again into one end of other wing, then into far end of same joint (leaving a stitch showing 1–2 inches long, depending on size of wing) and pass back through body and out at corresponding part of the first wing.

3 Tie the two thread ends into a bow.

4 Re-thread needle, insert through fleshy skin at end of one drumstick, through the gristle on each side of the pope's nose, and out through skin of other drumstick end.

5 Re-insert needle into carcass under drumsticks; draw through.

6 Tie the two thread ends firmly at side.

To truss with a skewer

Push skewer through bird below thigh bone, turn onto its breast. Catch in the wing pinions, pass string under ends of skewer and cross pinions over its back. Turn bird over, bring up string to secure drumsticks and tie around pope's nose.

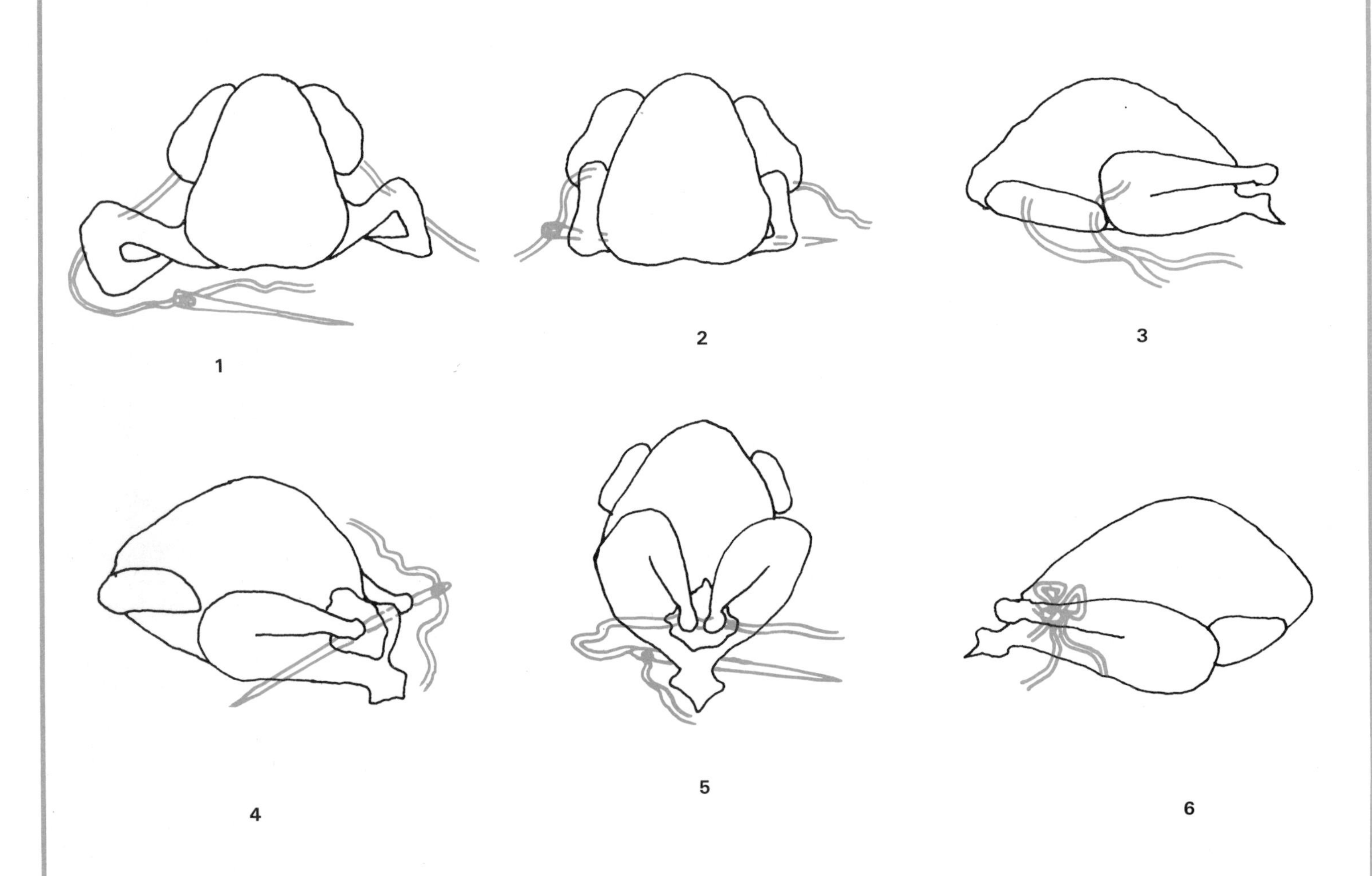

Carving a cooked chicken

1 Hold bird firmly with carving fork down through back. Cut skin around leg, place knife between leg and carcass and press gently outwards to break thigh joint. Cut through, slipping the knife point under back to release the oyster (choice meat lying on each side of the backbone) with thigh.

2 With knife at top end of breastbone opposite where breast and wishbone meet, cut down parallel to one side of wishbone to include a good slice of breast with wing. Sever wing joint.
3 and **4** Carve similar pieces from other side of bird, then remove wishbone by slicing behind it, down front of carcass. Carve remaining breast into 2–4 even slices, depending on size of bird. With a large chicken, divide leg in two through joint, leaving a good portion of thigh meat with drumstick. Trim protruding bones using half-hole in scissors or poultry shears.

Accompaniments to Entrée

Julienne Potato Cake

1 lb potatoes, peeled
2 tablespoons butter
salt and pepper

6–7 inch skillet or heavy frying pan

The potatoes may be peeled ahead of time, but they must not be cut into strips until just before using. Soaking in water removes a certain amount of the starch needed to knit them together, but if the potatoes are soaked whole, the loss will not be too great. As they cook the steam and starch combine and, when tender, the potato cake is easy to remove from the pan.

Method
Cut peeled potatoes into julienne strips and dry thoroughly in a cloth or paper towel. Rub the butter in a thick, even coating over base and sides of pan and press in the potatoes, seasoning only when a thick layer covers the base (salt makes the potatoes stick).
Watchpoint: do not add too much salt as all the seasoning will be absorbed by the potatoes.

If the pan has no close-fitting lid, put an overlapping layer of buttered foil between pan and a lid or heatproof plate to prevent loss of steam, or the potatoes will burn on the bottom before they are tender. When cooking them on top of the stove, use a gentle, even heat and allow about 30–40 minutes.

However, when entertaining, it is easier to combine top of stove and oven heat as follows. Cook potatoes for 10–15 minutes on top of the stove on a steady heat, testing for browning by lifting the lid and inserting a palette knife down the side so you can take a quick look. With experience your nose will tell you when the potatoes are browned by the unmistakable smell of beurre noisette (butter cooked to a nut brown). Transfer the pan to the oven and continue cooking at 400°F for 30 minutes or until potatoes are very tender (test them with the point of a knife). To serve, turn out the cake in a dish.

To make larger quantities for serving more than 4–6 people, use 2 pans.

Julienne potato cake is turned out and served brown side up

The term **julienne** can mean either a clear vegetable soup (consommé julienne) to which a mixture of shredded cooked vegetables has been added, or can refer to the cut size and shape of vegetables and garnishes for certain dishes. A julienne strip is usually about $\frac{1}{8}$–$\frac{1}{4}$ inch thick by $1\frac{1}{2}$–2 inches long, as with this julienne potato cake.

Green Salad

The classic accompaniment to a French roast chicken is a green salad mixed with a vinaigrette dressing and generously sprinkled with chopped herbs and parsley.

Green salad can be made of plain lettuce – romaine, Boston, Bibb, field, or iceberg, depending on the season – or can be a mixture of other green vegetables such as watercress, sliced cucumber, sliced avocado and scallions. Chicory, endive and escarole can also be added when available, but vegetables such as tomatoes or beets are best served separately.

It is most important to prepare salad correctly. Lettuce leaves should be carefully detached and the coarse outside ones discarded. Use a stainless steel knife (not a steel knife) to trim the bottom stalk or to quarter the hearts as garnish. If the leaves are large, tear apart rather than cut them. Wash them well, then swing dry in a salad basket or pat them in paper towels or a clean dish towel. This must be done thoroughly or the water will dilute the dressing and the salad will taste insipid. If the lettuce is limp, chill it in the vegetable drawer of the refrigerator.

Watercress should be well rinsed in the bunch under cold water, then shaken to remove the moisture. Carefully pick over the leaves and remove some of the stalk, but if this is clean and free from little hairs, do not discard it. These stalks can be snipped into small pieces with scissors and used with chopped herbs, scattered over vegetable soups as a garnish, or added to savory butters. They have a pleasant, slightly peppery taste.

Garlic must be used with caution in a green salad. Add a very little garlic to the dressing or rub the salad bowl with a peeled clove. Better still, rub a clove over a crust of French or regular bread to make what is called a chapon. Then put the salad in the bowl and bury the chapon among the leaves. It is tossed with the dressing, but should be removed before the salad is served.

A green salad should be tossed with dressing at the last moment, otherwise the leaves will wilt and become unappetizing. It is easiest to mix a large amount of salad with its dressing in an oversize bowl before transferring it to a salad bowl.

However, there is a way to dress a salad so the leaves remain crisp for slightly longer. Sprinkle only the oil over the salad to make the leaves glisten. Mix the vinegar with seasonings in a bowl, adding garlic if you like, and sprinkle this over the salad. Just before serving, toss the salad well so the dressing is evenly distributed, always taste the salad before serving to see if more seasoning is needed.

Salad ingredients include from left to right, front: Bulb of garlic, Belgian endive, field lettuce, cucumber, avocado, scallions. Back: escarole, Bibb and Boston lettuce

Vinaigrette Dressing

1 tablespoon vinegar (any of the following types: red or white wine, cider or tarragon)
3 tablespoons oil, preferably olive or peanut
$\frac{1}{4}$ teaspoon salt
$\frac{1}{4}$ teaspoon black pepper, freshly ground
chopped fresh herbs (thyme, marjoram, basil, or parsley – optional)

Method

Mix the vinegar with seasonings and gradually add the oil, whisking until the dressing thickens slightly. Taste it for the correct seasoning – add more salt if the dressing is sharp yet oily.

Fresh herbs are an excellent addition as is a pinch of sugar, according to your taste.

Strictly speaking, **vinaigrette dressing** is made of oil and vinegar flavored with herbs, while a plain mixture of oil and vinegar is called a French dressing. However, in this Cooking Course, both dressings will be referred to as vinaigrette to avoid confusion with the tomato-flavored commercial French dressing.

Seasoning. Unless other flavorings are mentioned, 'to season' always means to add salt and pepper to a mixture. To obtain the right balance of flavors, it is essential to taste a mixture, as the same foods may need different amounts of seasoning according to their kind.

Dessert

Mousse au Chocolat

6 squares (6 oz) semisweet chocolate
2–3 tablespoons water, or black coffee
1 tablespoon butter
1 tablespoon rum, or $\frac{1}{2}$ teaspoon vanilla
3 eggs
$\frac{1}{2}$ cup heavy cream (to serve – optional)

4–6 mousse or custard pots

Method
Break the chocolate into pieces, put into a small saucepan with the water or black coffee and stir continuously over gentle heat until melted and thick and creamy. The chocolate should be quite hot, but the sides of the pan must not become so hot that you cannot touch them. Remove from heat and stir in the butter and flavoring.

Separate the eggs, putting whites into a small bowl and dropping yolks, one at a time, into the chocolate pan; stir well after each addition.

Watchpoint: the chocolate should be hot enough so that when yolks are added, they cook slightly.

Beat the whites until they hold a soft peak and fold very carefully into the chocolate. When thoroughly mixed, pour mousse into the pots and chill overnight in the refrigerator. For easy pouring, transfer mixture first into a pitcher, scraping the pan with a rubber spatula.

These mousses may be served plain with the cigarettes Russes cookies or they may be topped with cream. Chill the cream, then stiffly whip it (take care not to overbeat or it will curdle) and add a spoonful to the top of each pot. Better still, put the cream into a pastry bag fitted with a star tube and pipe a flat rosette to cover the top of each pot. Just before serving, stick a cookie into the center of the cream.

To Pipe Whipped Cream

Use a pastry bag made of canvas or nylon with a waterproof finish. This is fitted with a star tube that has a $\frac{1}{2}$ inch opening.

Whip the cream until it is stiff but still falls from a spoon – if it is too stiff, it will curdle as it is forced through the tube.

To pipe a rosette: hold the pastry bag upright in one hand, and using the other hand to guide the nozzle, move the tube in a clockwise circle, pressing the pastry bag firmly and continuously.

To pipe a flower shape: hold the pastry bag upright and press gently; when the flower is of the right size, lift the bag away.

To save wasting cream, practice piping with a pastry bag filled with cooked mashed potato.

Accompaniment to Dessert

Cigarettes Russes

2 egg whites
$\frac{1}{2}$ cup sugar
$\frac{1}{4}$ cup butter
$1\frac{1}{2}$ tablespoons flour
$\frac{1}{2}$ teaspoon vanilla

Makes 24 cigarettes.

Method
Grease and flour a baking sheet and set oven at moderate (350°F).

With a fork, beat egg whites until frothy in a bowl, add sugar and beat until smooth. Melt the butter and stir into mixture with the flour. Add the vanilla and spread single tablespoons of mixture into 4 X 3 inch rectangles on prepared baking sheet. Bake for 5–6 minutes in heated oven.

Watchpoint: it is a good idea to test the mixture by baking only one cookie at first. If difficult to roll up, add 1 teaspoon flour, or if too firm and hard add 2 teaspoons of melted butter to the mixture.

Take the cookies from the oven, cool 1–2 seconds and remove from baking sheet with a sharp knife, placing them upside down on the table. Quickly roll each one tightly around a wooden spoon handle, skewer, or pencil, holding it firmly in the hand (see photograph, right). Remove cookie at once from spoon and cool on a wire rack. If cookies become too hard to roll, put them back in the oven for 1–2 minutes to soften. Store in an airtight tin.

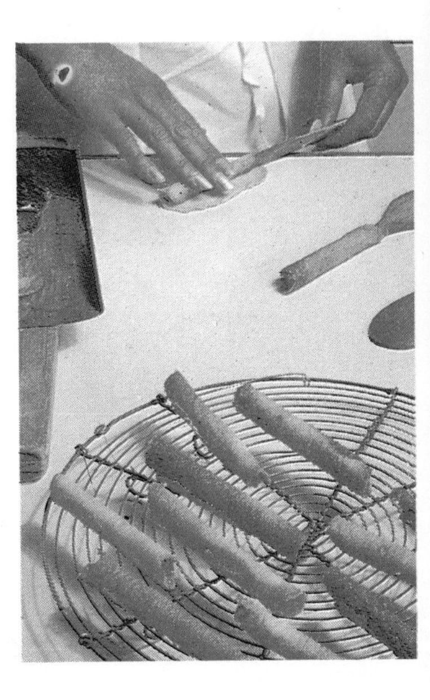

To shape the cigarette cookies, roll each one carefully around a wooden spoon handle. See finished cigarettes Russes on opposite page.

Individual mousses au chocolat are topped with whipped cream and served with cigarettes Russes

HOW TO ROAST

Most cooks think of roasting as cooking in the oven with the meat set in a roasting pan but true roasting is done on a revolving spit over an open fire. However, few home kitchens are equipped with the modern mechanical equivalent of the traditional spit and results are equally good by the oven method, although the meat does not have the same flavor as meat cooked over charcoal. More care is needed during oven cooking, for the meat is baked in dry heat rather than roasted and can easily become tough and hard if it is not basted often.

The task of choosing meat has been greatly simplified by the Department of Agriculture, which grades most meat sold with a purple stamp. For roasting and broiling, buy the best cut and the highest grade you can find, because meat that is cooked at high heat quickly becomes tough if not liberally marbled with fat. For braising and pot roasting, take your choice – flavor will be better in the better grades. Use lowest grades of meat only for making soup.

If in doubt about the merits of a cut of meat, pot roast or braise rather than oven roast it.

Regular Roasting Times for Meat

	Total cooking time (all at 375°F Oven Temperature)	Temperature on meat thermometer
Beef	Rare: 15 minutes per lb plus 15 minutes more	140°F
	Medium: 18 minutes per lb plus 20 minutes more	160°F
	Well Done: 20 minutes per lb plus 30 minutes more	170°F
Lamb	Medium: 18 minutes per lb plus 18 minutes more	160°F
	Well done: 20 minutes per lb plus 20 minutes more	175°F
Pork	25 minutes per lb plus 25 minutes more	170°F
Veal	Well done: 25 minutes per lb plus 25 minutes more	175°F

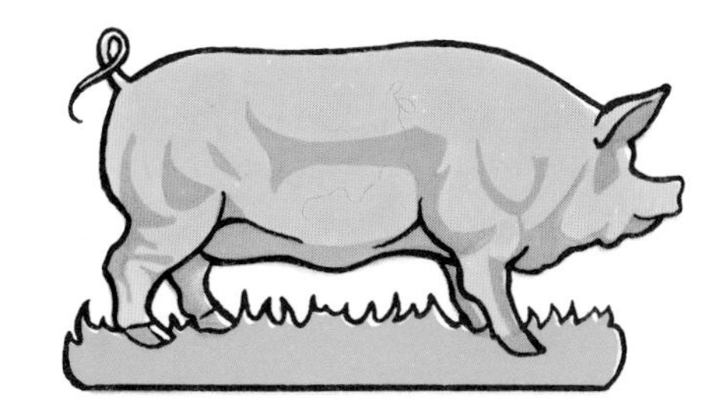

The amount of meat you need depends on the number and appetites of the people you are cooking for, and on the other courses included in the menu. As a rough guide, 1 lb of lean meat with no bone, like fillet of beef, should serve three people. The fatter the cut and the more bone included, the fewer people it will serve, so that 1 lb of spareribs or lamb shoulder on the bone is scarcely enough for one.

There are several schools of thought about roasting meat, particularly beef. The French like to roast at a high temperature to seal in the juices, but some cooks prefer a low heat to avoid shrinkage. We favor a compromise of moderate temperatures for roasting with the exception of beef fillet which needs special treatment (see page 29).

The best procedure for roasting is as follows:

1 Remove the meat from the refrigerator 30 minutes before cooking – all meat for roasting should be at room temperature.

2 Preheat the oven to the correct temperature, first checking that the shelf is in position – this varies with the type of oven, so follow the manufacturer's instructions carefully.

3 Put the roasting pan in the oven with 2–4 tablespoons oil or shortening, or, better still, drippings saved from a previous roast of the same kind. The exact amount of fat needed depends on the size of the cut.

4 When the fat is sizzling, set the meat in the pan, putting fatty cuts on a rack so they are drained during cooking. Baste well with oil to seal in the juices and return to the oven. If you do not use a rack, place the cut on its edge rather than flat on the outside, since the surface in contact with the pan may get hard and overcook. This is particularly important with a round cut like boned rib of beef.

5 Cook according to the weight and thickness of the meat (see chart on page 26), basting every 15–20 minutes to keep the meat moist and tender. If possible, test temperature with a meat thermometer inserted before cooking begins into the center of the meat, not near a bone. This is the most reliable method. The temperatures given below are registered when the meat is still in the oven; the cut will continue cooking for 10–15 minutes after it is removed and the temperatures may rise by as much as 10°F.

6 When the meat is cooked, it should be put on a carving board or platter and kept warm. Plan the cooking time so the meat stands for 15 minutes while the gravy is prepared and the vegetables finish cooking. This allows the meat to 'set' so that it is easier to carve and loses less juice.

7 A roast needs good gravy: strong and clear for beef, mutton and lamb, and lightly thickened for pork and veal. Serve the gravy separately.

Veal and special roast meat dishes will be discussed in a future Volume, as well as carving meat, and rotisserie and slow oven roasting.

Grades of Meat

Prime: fine-textured meat, bright red and marbled with fat to give flavor and tenderness.

Choice: the best grade generally available; it has less marbling of fat and is slightly darker in color.

Good: reliable in quality, although it has less fat and juiciness than the top grades.

Standard: young, low quality meat – it has little fat and poor flavor.

Commercial and Utility: lean meat from old animals.

BEEF FOR ROASTING

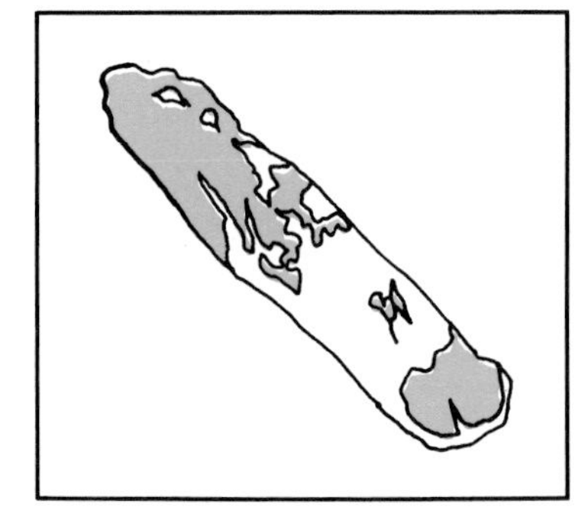

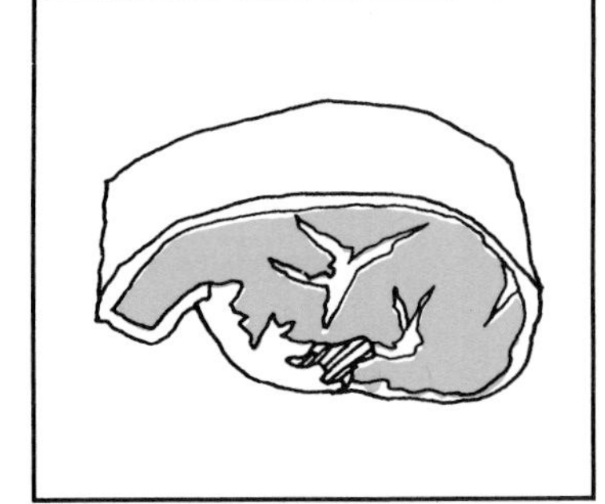

Opinions vary on how long a cut of beef should be matured, but most connoisseurs agree that purplish-red meat which is well aged has more flavor than bright-red, freshly killed meat. The fat on the cut should be firm in texture and creamy in color, and the lean meat should be marbled with fat.

Ideally, when cooked, roast beef should be a delicate deep shade of pink inside, and a crisp, dark brown on the outside. The best cuts for roasting are rib, the fillet, and the English cut of sirloin which includes some fillet. The top grades of rump and sirloin tip can also be roasted.

If serving cold roast beef with a salad, try to allow time for the cooked meat to cool before carving it, otherwise it tends to lose color and flavor and is less juicy (also applies to other cold meats like lamb and pork).

Fillet or Tenderloin

The fillet is taken from the ribs of the animal and is the most tender cut. It weighs 3–6 lb, and as this is the total weight of fillet in a carcass of 600–700 lb, it is in great demand and is very expensive. However, you need make no allowance for wastage as a well-trimmed fillet is solid lean meat. For roasting it is often barded by the butcher, i.e. wrapped around with a thin layer of fat. Alternatively, strips of fat may be sewn into the meat to add richness – this is called larding.

Sirloin Roast

To be a really good cut, the sirloin should not weigh less than 5 lb. It is a piece similar to the rib although it is cut nearer the hindquarter of the animal and includes part of the fillet. It is best cooked on the bone and needs regular basting as it is laid on its side in the pan, rather than stood upright. French butchers will offer you the contrefilet or entrecôte which is a compact, well-trimmed, and somewhat expensive cut from the top of the sirloin.

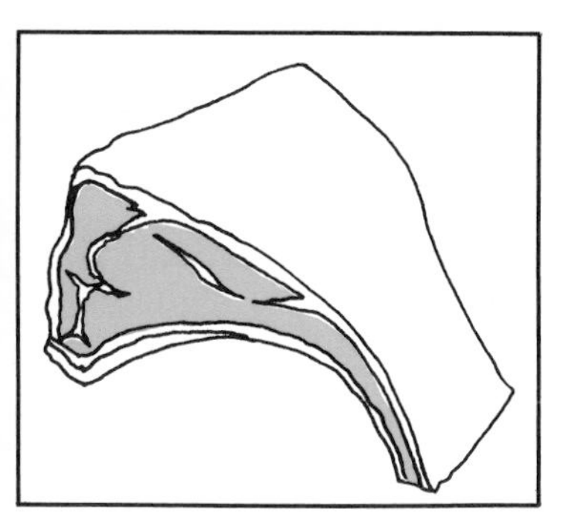

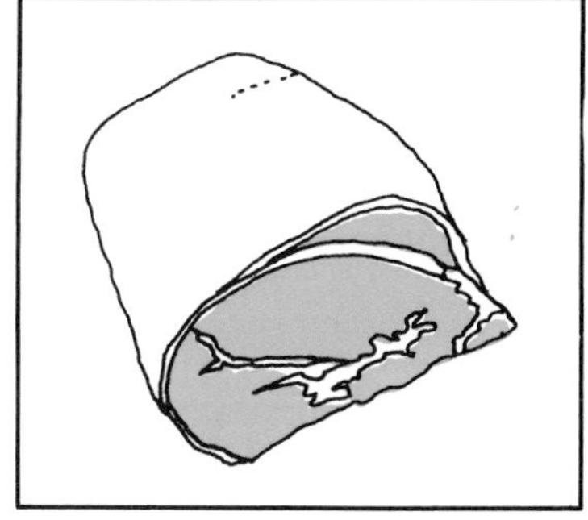

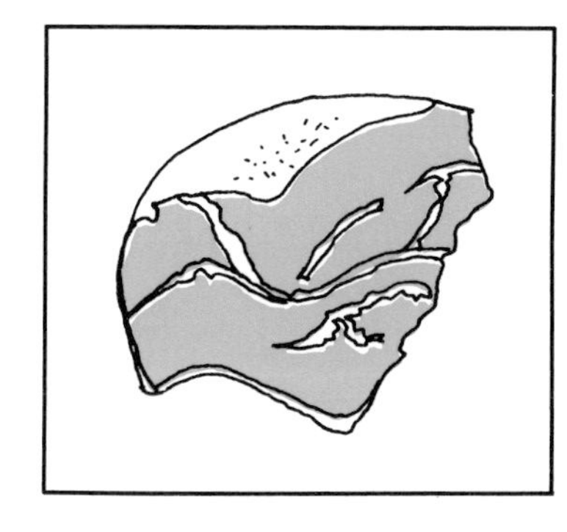

Rib Roast

The rib has an incomparably rich flavor and is almost as tender as fillet. As many as seven ribs may be included, but the first three are the best (two ribs form the minimum piece for roasting). The cut weighs at least 4 lb and is often sold boned and rolled for easy carving, but is at its finest when cooked on the bone to reduce shrinkage and retain the flavor. It should be cooked standing upright on its bones so that the layer of top fat automatically bastes the meat beneath. **Shell of beef** is sometimes cut from the rib, and consists of all the lean meat without bones or fat. It looks like a large fillet.

Sirloin Tip

The sirloin tip is, in fact, part of the round of beef, not the sirloin. It is a triangular cut, weighing about 9 lb, and makes a good family roast when of top quality. The lower grades should be pot roasted.

Rump

A rump of top grade beef makes an excellent, less expensive roast. It contains a good deal of bone and waste, so normally it is boned and rolled. Even so, it is a large cut, weighing up to 12 lb and is often divided into two or more pieces. The fat should be flattened so it covers the surface of the meat to keep it moist during cooking.

Roasting a beef fillet

A fillet of beef should be cooked for a relatively short time at a high temperature so that it is crisply brown on the outside and rare in the middle. Preheat oven to hot (400°F). In a roasting pan heat 2–3 tablespoons oil or drippings; when sizzling, add fillet, baste with fat, turn and baste again. Lift meat onto a rack, stand it in the roasting pan and roast in the heated oven, allowing 40 minutes for a 2 lb fillet, and 15 minutes per lb for larger cuts. Baste meat every 15 minutes and turn over when half cooked. Stand in a warm place for 15 minutes before carving and make the gravy as for other roasts of beef.

TO SERVE WITH BEEF ROASTS

Yorkshire Pudding

1 cup flour
½ teaspoon salt
2 eggs
1 cup water mixed with ½ cup milk
2 tablespoons beef drippings

Method

Sift the flour with the salt into a bowl. Make a well in the center and add the eggs with half the milk and water. With a whisk, stir carefully, gradually drawing in all the flour to form a smooth batter. Add half the remaining liquid and beat for 3 minutes. Then add rest of liquid, cover, and stand in a cool place (not the refrigerator) for at least 1 hour before cooking. Resting the batter before cooking it softens the starch and breaks down any 'rubberiness' to give a lighter pudding.

Heat 2 tablespoons drippings from the roast beef on top of the stove in a shallow 8 X 12 inch cake pan or in 12 individual muffin pans, tilting to coat the sides of the pans with the hot fat. Add the batter to a depth of about ½ inch and bake in a very hot oven (425°F–450°F) or on a shelf above the meat. The small puddings need a higher heat than the large one and are cooked when puffed and brown – about 20 minutes. The large pudding will take 30–40 minutes.

Horseradish Cream

2 tablespoons freshly grated horseradish root or ¼ cup prepared horseradish
2 teaspoons white wine vinegar
1 teaspoon dry mustard
1 teaspoon sugar (or to taste)
pinch of salt
black pepper, freshly ground
½ cup heavy cream

Method

Combine vinegar and seasonings and then add the horseradish. Whip the cream until it holds a soft shape and mix gently into the other ingredients. Chill.

When fresh horseradish is not available, add whipped cream to prepared horseradish and season to taste, adding very little vinegar.

Yorkshire pudding takes its name from a county in the north of England where it was the custom to cook a pudding under the Sunday roast which had been placed on a rack. All the drippings fell through the rack and the pudding became saturated with the rich and satisfying flavor of roasted meat.

To take the edge off hearty appetites, the pudding was served in slices with gravy before the meat.

Cabbage

Cooked cabbage is much maligned and a Grand Diplôme cook should remember the following rules:

1 Cabbage, like all vegetables that grow above the ground, must be put into plenty of boiling salted water and cooked uncovered.

2 Remove the coarse outer leaves, quarter the cabbage, cut out the hard stem and finely shred the leaves. Wash it all thoroughly.

3 Avoid overcooking. For plain boiling, 5–6 minutes is enough. Although the cabbage must be tender, it should still have a certain bite and crispness. After draining, finish cooking by tossing over heat with melted butter.

4 Avoid keeping cabbage hot for any length of time because this gives an unpleasant odor and spoils its color. Cook it early by all means, but when tender, tip it into a colander, drain and rinse well with cold water. When almost ready to serve, turn cabbage into a shallow pan, heat quickly until steam stops rising, then add butter in small pieces and toss until melted. Season with salt and plenty of black pepper and serve at once.

Buttered Squash

1½ lb yellow or crookneck squash, or zucchini
3–4 tablespoons butter
1 tablespoon salt and pepper
chopped parsley (for garnish)

Method

Wash squash or zucchini and cut in ½ inch slices, discarding stalk and flower ends. Melt butter in a large shallow pan and add squash. Season, cover with buttered foil and lid, and cook over low heat (15–20 minutes or until tender), shaking the pan from time to time. Sprinkle with parsley before serving.

Glazed Carrots

1–1½ lb carrots
1 teaspoon sugar
2 tablespoons butter
salt
chopped fresh mint (for garnish)

Method

Peel carrots and quarter them or leave them whole, if small. If very large, cut in thin slices. Put in a saucepan with water to cover, sugar, butter and a pinch of salt. Cover and simmer until tender, then remove lid and boil until all the water has evaporated – the butter and sugar forms a shiny glaze over carrots. Just before serving, sprinkle with mint.

Creamed Turnips

1–1½ lb small turnips
2 tablespoons butter
black pepper
½ cup heavy cream

Method

Peel turnips, quarter them, and cook, covered, in plenty of boiling salted water until tender. Drain well and return to the heat for a few minutes to dry. Crush with a fork or a potato masher, add butter and stir over low heat until all the water has evaporated. Season with plenty of pepper and add cream immediately before serving.

Roast rib of beef, rare in the center brown outside, served with roast potatoes and buttered squash

Roast Potatoes

Choose medium white or baking potatoes of even size. Peel, and halve them if they are large. Blanch by putting into cold salted water and bringing to a boil. Drain, and scratch the surfaces lightly with a fork. (This ensures a crisp brittle outside after roasting.) Put the potatoes in the same pan as the meat (the fat should be sizzling hot) 40–45 minutes before the meat is cooked and baste well. Cook until soft (test with a cooking fork or fine skewer), basting the potatoes at the same time as the meat and turning them after 25 minutes. Drain on paper towels, pile in a serving dish and sprinkle with a little salt. Do not cover before serving or potatoes will become soggy.

Ideally, roast beef should be a delicate deep shade of pink inside

Gravy

The base of a good gravy is the sediment left in the roasting pan to which stock is added to dissolve and augment the juices.

To make stock, simmer the knuckle bone from the leg or shoulder (or the chine bone from the loin) or ask the meat man for a beef or veal bone. Add with onion, carrot, a little salt and pepper, and water to cover. Cover the pan and simmer at least 1 hour before straining the stock into the roasting pan. When no bone is available, use canned bouillon instead of stock, but do not add seasoning without first tasting the gravy.

To make gravy itself, remove meat and tilt the roasting pan gently to pour away the fat or skim off the fat with a metal spoon while retaining the juices and sediment at the bottom. Sprinkle pan with just enough flour to absorb the small quantity of fat remaining (2 teaspoons flour is usually enough for 1½ cups gravy), and brown this flour slowly over medium heat, stirring and scraping the pan to remove sediment from sides.

Stir in 1½–2 cups stock, bring to a boil and season with salt and pepper. Boil gravy to reduce it to 1–1½ cups and to concentrate the flavor. Strain into a gravy boat and serve very hot.

Good gravy should be a deep rich brown, particularly for beef. This depends mainly on the color of the juices after the meat is cooked, but a pallid gravy can be darkened if you brown the flour thoroughly before adding stock to the pan. In a thin roasting pan, take care not to scorch the flour while browning it.

LAMB FOR ROASTING

Lamb is graded like beef and the highest quality meat is clear pink with white fat. The size of the carcass varies with the breed of lamb, but the best is small. In spring it is possible to find baby lamb, especially in European-style markets, and this is a real delicacy. Many people like to cook lamb until it is well done. Younger lamb, however, has a much better flavor if cooked only until it is pink in the center (although not as rare as beef).

In France, roast lamb is served simply with gravy, generally accompanied by green beans and a baked potato dish called boulangère. The British like to add mint sauce or red currant jelly, and here mint jelly is a favorite accompaniment.

There are other ways of turning plain lamb roast into a roast with a subtle difference. You can insert a few small pieces of peeled garlic clove by the leg shank bone, or simply rub the meat with a cut clove of garlic. Try sprinkling fresh chopped rosemary on top or placing a sprig of fresh rosemary under the cut before roasting.

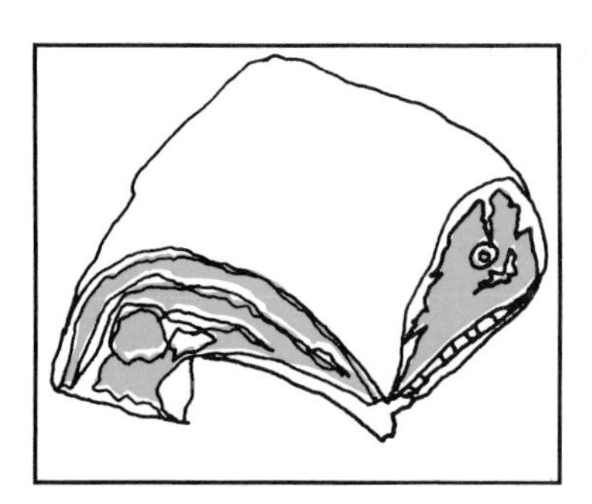

Shoulder

The shoulder is an awkward cut since it contains three bones set at different angles. For roasting, the simplest method is to have it boned and rolled or boned and tied flat as a cushion roast, when it is ideal for stuffing. This is a relatively inexpensive, juicy cut, although it can be fatty.

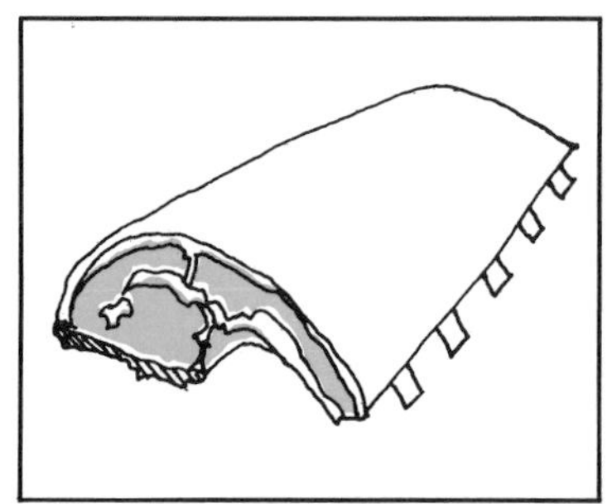

Rack

Rack is an excellent, if expensive small cut for roasting, and generally weighs about $2\frac{1}{2}$ lb. Have the butcher remove the chine bone and cut the fat from the top of the rib bones to a depth of $1\frac{1}{2}$–2 inches, so that the bones can be scraped clean. If you like, the surface of the fat can be scored in a lattice pattern. To make something special of a rack, you can prepare a carré d'agneau. Instructions for preparing this cut yourself will be given in a future Volume.

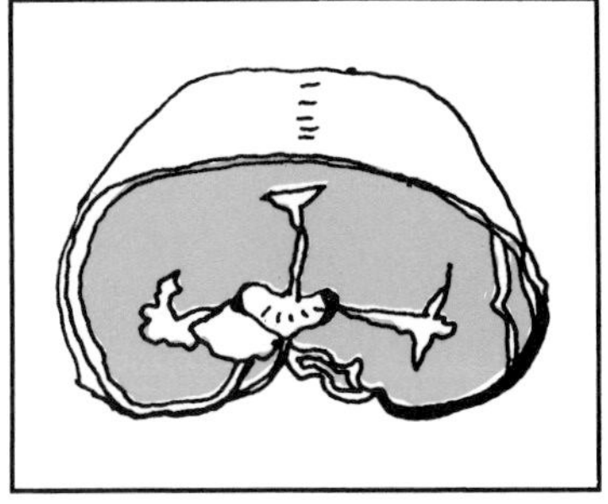

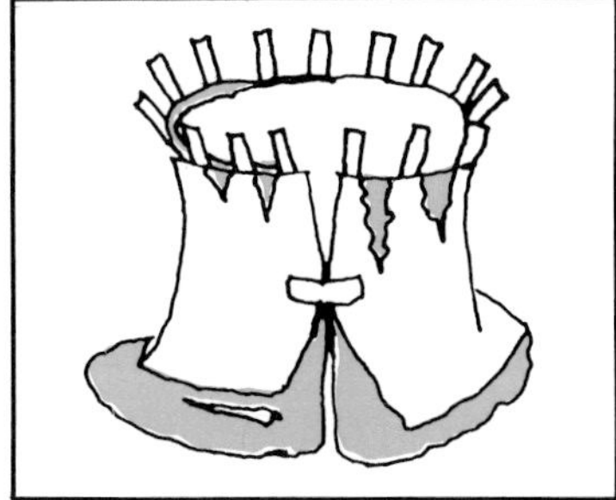

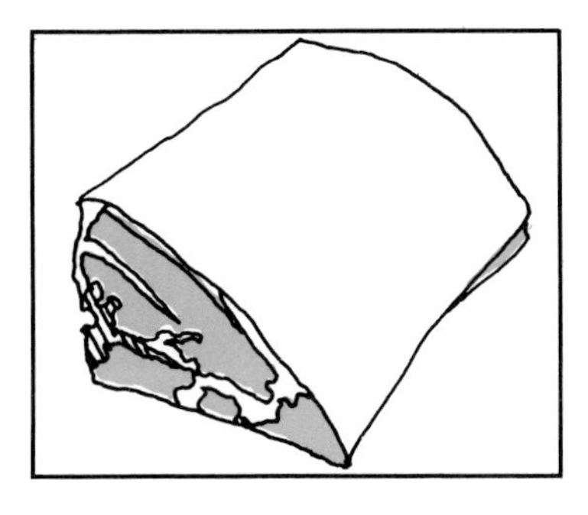

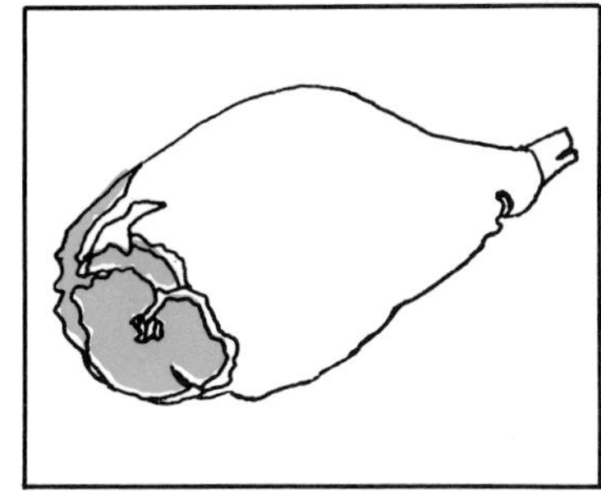

Saddle

The saddle is the double loin, often sold rolled, with the rib bones removed. Its weight averages 5 lb and this will serve 6 people.

Crown Roast

The butcher will prepare this impressive roast from two racks of lamb by sewing them together so they form a circle with the ribs pointing up and out. The center may be stuffed before cooking (allow at least 30 minutes extra time in the oven) or filled with spring vegetables before serving. Crown the rib bones with paper frills. Instructions for preparing this cut yourself will be given in a future Volume.

Loin

The leanest, sweetest chops are cut from the loin portion of lamb and, when left whole as a roast, the loin is also a choice cut. Carving is easier if the backbone is chined so it can be cut out after cooking, rather than each rib bone being chopped apart.

Leg

This is the leanest cut so it must be well basted during roasting. The weight can vary from 3–8 lb, depending on the size of the animal and whether some of the loin chops are included with the leg.

If ordered in advance, a butcher can obtain a **baron of lamb**, the whole hindquarter. This is only practical for a home kitchen when cut from a baby lamb.

Another unusual cut is the **sirloin**, a boned, rolled piece taken from a cross-section of the carcass at the top of the leg. It should be cooked like a boned saddle of lamb.

A roast rack of lamb is one of the luxury cuts; it should be well trimmed and scored on the surface

TO SERVE WITH LAMB ROASTS

Buttered Green Beans

1 lb green beans
2 tablespoons butter
salt and pepper
chopped parsley (for garnish)

Method

If beans are small, wash them, snip off the ends and leave them whole. If they are large, cut in two or three or 'French' them by cutting in fine, diagonal slices. If at all limp, soak them in iced water for 1 hour before cutting and cooking.

Bring a large pan of salted water to a boil, add the beans and boil uncovered over high heat for 15 minutes or until tender. Drain and run under cold water to set the color. Melt the butter in the saucepan, add the beans and toss over the heat until they are very hot and coated with butter. Add pepper to taste and sprinkle with chopped parsley before serving. The beans may be boiled up to an hour in advance and reheated to serve in the butter.

Petits Pois à la Française

3–4 cups shelled fresh peas
1 romaine lettuce, shredded
10–12 scallions, cut in 2 inch pieces
2 teaspoons sugar
bouquet garni
$\frac{1}{4}$ cup butter
$\frac{1}{2}$ cup cold water
salt

Method

Put the peas in a saucepan with the lettuce, scallions, sugar, bouquet garni and half the butter; add the water. Cover pan with a heatproof plate, half-filled with cold water, and cook quickly for 20–25 minutes or until peas are tender.

Watchpoint: cold water on top of the pan condenses steam as it rises and keeps peas moist during cooking. Add more cold water as water in plate evaporates.

Just before serving, remove bouquet garni and add remaining butter with salt to taste. Shake pan well to mix and serve in a hot dish.

Add scallion pieces to peas and shredded lettuce for petits pois à la Française

Mint Sauce

$\frac{1}{2}$ cup fresh mint leaves tightly packed
6 tablespoons sugar
$\frac{1}{4}$ cup boiling water
wine vinegar to taste
pinch of salt

Mint sauce should be bright green, smooth and pulpy, not liquid.

Method

Strip mint leaves from stem, chop finely, and pound with sugar until smooth. Add boiling water to improve color and melt sugar. Add wine vinegar to taste and season with salt.

Kneaded Butter (beurre manié)

This is a liaison or a mixture used for thickening liquids. Work softened butter with half as much flour into a paste on a plate with a fork and add in small pieces to the warm mixture to be thickened, away from the heat. Stir, shake the pan and reboil. If still not thick enough, add more as before. As the kneaded butter melts, it distributes the flour in the liquid.

Boulangère Potatoes

$1\frac{1}{2}$ lb potatoes
3 medium onions, sliced
salt and pepper
1 bay leaf
$1\frac{1}{2}$ cups stock
1 tablespoon meat drippings or oil

Method

Blanch the onions by putting them in cold water, bringing to a boil and boiling 1 minute before draining. Peel and slice potatoes thinly and arrange at once in layers with onions in a shallow ovenproof dish, seasoning each layer with salt and pepper. Add the bay leaf with enough stock to cover potatoes, dot with drippings or oil and bake in a hot oven (400°F) for 1 hour or until potatoes are soft and well browned.

Halfway through cooking, if the top layer of potatoes has curled, press it down into the stock with a spoon and add a little more drippings. If necessary, add more stock – the potatoes should be soft and moist when cooked, but not wet.

The name **boulangère** (baker) for this recipe has an ancient origin. Years ago, in country districts of France, small houses had no ovens, so the Sunday lunch of leg of lamb was set in a copper dish with sliced potatoes and onions around it. This was left at the local bakers to be cooked while the family went on their way to church. After Mass, the dish would be collected hot and cooked to perfection for the midday meal.

PORK FOR ROASTING

The flesh of good pork is fine-grained and firm, with white fat and pinkish lean meat, and in general the darker the meat, the older the animal. Don't let the butcher trim away too much fat as this adds flavor.

Pork is a rich meat, so it is a good idea to serve an accompaniment that is refreshing and sharp. Traditionally, this is in the form of baked apples or apple sauce, or many people enjoy apricots, pineapple, or cranberry sauce as an accompaniment.

Pork must always be thoroughly cooked to prevent danger of infection which may be present in the raw meat. Juices that run from meat after cooking should be clear – not pink, which indicates undercooking – and a meat thermometer should register at least 170°F before the roast is taken from the oven.

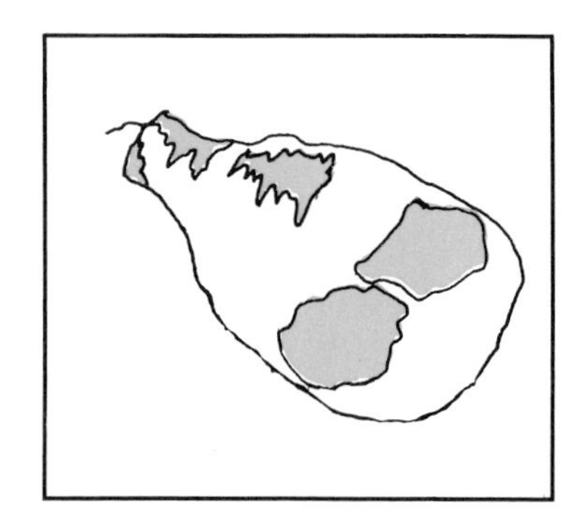

Fresh Ham or Leg of Pork

This is a large cut averaging 12 lb and it is often divided, like a cured ham, into butt and shank halves. The shank or the whole ham can be boned by the butcher for stuffing.

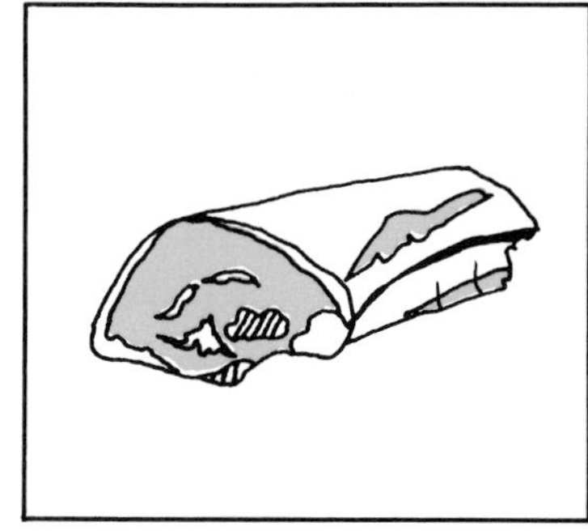

Sirloin

The sirloin cut of pork runs along the backbone from the ham to the loin. The bone structure is complicated so you will do best to buy pork sirloin ready boned and rolled rather than attempting to carve it from the bone.

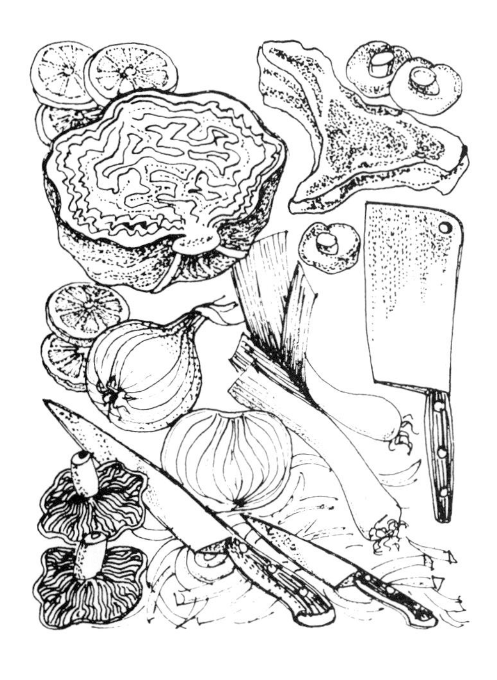

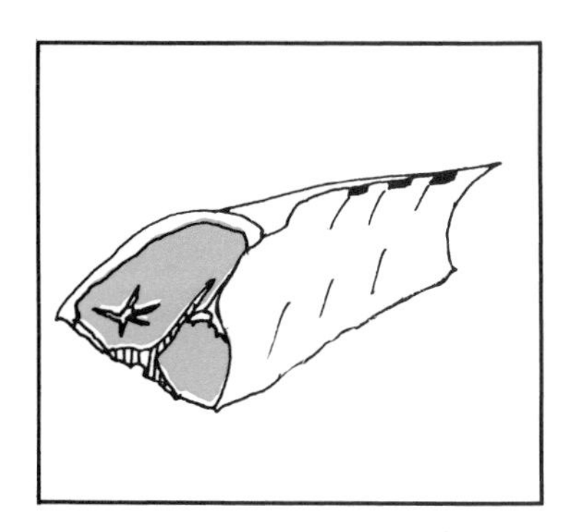

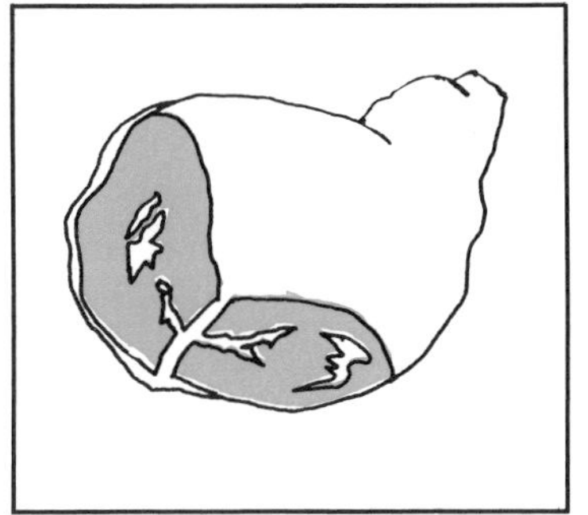

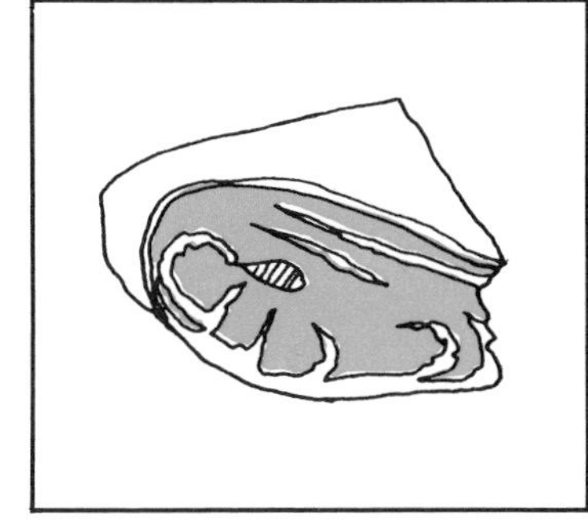

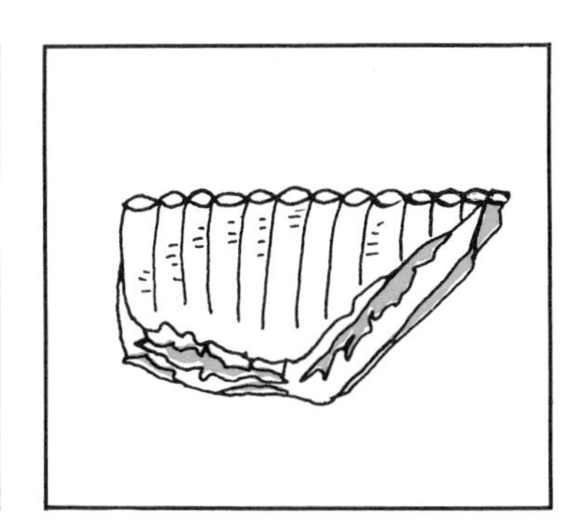

Loin

Loin is the choicest pork roast and it varies in size according to how many ribs are included. The center cut is the best since it contains part of the tenderloin.

A **crown roast** of pork can be made with 10 or more of the loin ribs. It looks like a crown roast of lamb and the center can be stuffed or filled with vegetables in the same way.

Picnic Shoulder

The shoulder of a very small pig may be left whole, but generally it is divided into the picnic shoulder and the Boston butt. Both the whole and the half picnic shoulder are easiest to cope with when boned and rolled, or stuffed and sewn flat in cushion style.

Boston Butt

Like picnic shoulder, the meat of Boston butt is juicy and tender, but it is hard to carve it from the bone; buy it boned and rolled if possible.

Spareribs

Spareribs are what remain when all the other cuts of pork have been removed, but no one thinks of them as a reject. The meat is some of the most succulent on the pig and is excellent roasted, whether or not the ribs are basted with a barbecue sauce. Cook them on a rack in a moderate oven (350°F) for 1 hour or more, allowing plenty of time for the fat to crisp and turning them so they brown evenly.

A pork shoulder with some of the favorite ingredients used for its accompaniments such as apples, onions and lemons

TO SERVE WITH PORK ROASTS

Apple Sauce

1 lb tart apples
rind from ½ lemon, thinly pared
2–3 tablespoons water
1 tablespoon butter
2 teaspoons sugar or to taste

Method
Peel, core and slice the apples and put them with the lemon rind in a saucepan with the water. Cover tightly and cook over low heat for 15–18 minutes until pulpy, stirring occasionally. Beat with a wooden spoon until smooth, or purée in a blender, or work through a strainer. Stir in the butter and sugar to taste. Serve hot.

Sage and Onion Stuffing

3 medium onions, finely sliced
¼ cup butter
2 cups fresh breadcrumbs
2 teaspoons dried sage
1 tablespoon chopped parsley
salt and pepper
1 egg, beaten to mix, or 5–6 tablespoons milk

Method
Boil the onions for 8–10 minutes in salted water. Drain, and stir in the butter. Add the breadcrumbs and herbs, season highly with salt and pepper and mix lightly with enough beaten egg or milk to bind. If the cut of pork is not suitable for stuffing, put the mixture in a small ovenproof dish, baste with 1 tablespoon drippings from the meat and bake in a hot oven (400°F) for 30 minutes or until browned.

Fresh Breadcrumbs
The easiest way to make fresh breadcrumbs is in the blender. Cut sliced white bread into cubes, removing the crust. Reduce these to crumbs, 1–2 slices at a time, in the blender at a moderately high speed.

If you have no blender, the traditional way to make breadcrumbs is to rub stale pieces of bread through a flat, wire sieve.

Braised Leeks

6–8 medium leeks
2 tablespoons butter
salt and pepper

Method
Trim the leeks, make a deep cross cut in the top of each and wash thoroughly under running water. Blanch by putting into boiling, salted water for 1 minute, and drain well. Arrange in a buttered casserole, season, cover tightly and bake in a moderately low oven (325°F) for 45 minutes or until tender.

Spiced Prunes

1 lb large prunes
2½ cups freshly brewed strong tea
2 cups red wine vinegar
1 cup sugar
1 teaspoon mixed pickling spice
thinly peeled rind of 1 lemon

This recipe for spiced prunes can be eaten 24 hours after making.

Method
Soak prunes overnight in cold tea. Transfer them to a saucepan with half the liquid from soaking, reserving the rest. Cover pan and cook prunes for 10–15 minutes or until tender. Drain them and add cooking liquid to reserved liquid.

Boil the vinegar, sugar, spices and lemon rind, tied in a cheesecloth bag, in a pan for 5 minutes, add 1¼ cups juice from the prunes and bring just back to a boil.

Pack prunes in hot dry glasses. Discard cheesecloth bag, cover prunes with liquid and seal at once.

Candied Sweet Potatoes

6 sweet potatoes
¼ cup orange juice
1 tablespoon lemon juice
½ cup brown sugar
salt and pepper
3 tablespoons butter

Method
Cook sweet potatoes in boiling salted water for 15 minutes or until just tender, drain and slice them. Arrange potatoes overlapping in a shallow, buttered ovenproof dish. Pour on the fruit juices, sprinkle with sugar and salt and pepper and dot with butter. Bake in a hot oven (400°F) for 30 minutes or until crisp and brown.

Glazed Onions

18 small onions, peeled
salt
2–3 tablespoons butter
1 tablespoon sugar

Method
Place onions in a pan, cover with cold water, add salt and bring to a boil. Drain off the water, add the butter and sprinkle sugar over the onions. Cover pan and cook onions gently, shaking pan occasionally to prevent them from sticking, until they are tender and golden brown with caramelized sugar. This should take about 10 minutes.

Invite friends to an informal supper

Entertain your friends with ease this week and offer them an informal supper for which you can prepare everything ahead of time. Simply reheat the chowder; the ham may be served hot or cold, as you choose. For a guarantee of success, follow the Timetable on page 42.

A perfect accompaniment for the baked ham can be found among the light, golden wines of the southern Rhine. Those from the town of Nierstein, particularly, exhibit a lush bouquet and sweet taste. The California counterpart of the German Rheinhessen wines is the Sylvaner and, while somewhat softer in aroma and flavor, is their equal in charm.

Mussel Chowder

Hot or Cold Baked Ham

Raisin or Cumberland Sauce

Green Salad　　*Mashed Potatoes*

Oranges in Caramel

Brandy Snaps

White wine – Niersteiner (Rheinhessen)
or Sylvaner (California)

Oranges in caramel, sprinkled with shredded orange rind, are accompanied by brandy snaps filled with whipped cream

TIMETABLE

Day before
Soak and simmer ham. Cool and refrigerate, covered, overnight.
Make raisin *or Cumberland* sauce and refrigerate.
Make brandy snaps and store in airtight container.

Morning
Make mussel chowder and refrigerate, covered.
Wash potatoes, peel and leave whole in cold water (not in refrigerator).
Cover ham with sugar topping and set in roasting pan with cider poured around it. If serving cold, complete cooking, score or caramelize top and chill.
Wash lettuce for salad, dry and wrap in a cloth or plastic bag. Refrigerate. Make dressing.
Prepare oranges and arrange in a glass dish.
Make caramel sauce and cool. Set aside.

Assemble equipment for final cooking from 5:45 p.m. for supper around 7:30 p.m.

You will find that **cooking times** given in the individual recipes for these dishes have sometimes been adapted in the timetable to help you when cooking and serving them as a party meal.

Order of Work

5:45
Pour caramel sauce over oranges, add orange peel shreds, cover dish with plastic wrap and refrigerate.

6:15
If serving ham hot, turn on oven. Assemble platters and plates to be warmed. Take raisin *or Cumberland* sauce from refrigerator to allow to come to room temperature. Put ham into oven and baste well. Stiffly whip cream and fill brandy snaps. Arrange on a platter and chill.

6:40
Score or caramelize top of ham, arrange on a platter, cover with foil and return to the oven, turned down to low (200°F), to keep hot.

6:50
Start cooking potatoes.

7:10
Drain potatoes, mash them with butter, pour hot milk over, cover, and leave in a warm place.

7:25
Heat chowder, bringing it almost to a boil.
Reheat sauce if serving hot with ham.
Toss salad with dressing.

7:30
Serve chowder.

Appetizer

Mussel Chowder

1 can (9 oz) cooked mussels, drained
1 green pepper, chopped
$\frac{1}{4}$ lb salt pork, diced
1 large onion, chopped
1 stalk of celery, chopped
2 medium potatoes, diced
1 small bay leaf
2 cups water
salt and pepper
$2\frac{1}{2}$ cups milk
2 tablespoons flour
1 tablespoon chopped parsley (for garnish)

Method
Blanch green pepper by cooking it in boiling water for 1 minute; drain, rinse under cold water and drain again. In a large saucepan, fry pork over gentle heat, stirring, until it starts to brown. Add onion and celery and cook until golden brown. Then add green pepper, potatoes, bay leaf and water and bring to a boil. Season and simmer 10 minutes or until potatoes are tender. Remove from heat.

Gradually add $\frac{1}{2}$ cup milk to flour, stirring to form a smooth mixture; blend into chowder. Return to heat and stir until boiling. Heat remaining milk and add to chowder with the mussels. Simmer 4–5 minutes before serving. Scatter a little parsley over the soup in each serving bowl.

The term **chowder** covers many different soups. Some are thick like a stew and others, such as the tomato-flavored Manhattan clam chowder, are a broth of diced ingredients. Most chowders are based on fish, but there are also meat and vegetable chowders. Perhaps the most famous is Boston (or New England) clam chowder which is a rich, milk-based soup flavored simply with salt pork and onion.

Chowder was introduced to the U.S. by early French settlers, and the word originates either from 'chaudrée de Fouras', a fish soup from the Fouras region of France, or from 'chaudière' (kettle).

An Informal Supper

A little chopped parsley is scattered over individual bowls of mussel chowder just before serving

Baked ham is more appetizing with its sugar crust scored in decorative lines

Entrée

Baked Ham

2–4 lb piece of country ham
1 onion, peeled and quartered
1 carrot, quartered
1 stalk of celery
large bouquet garni
6 peppercorns

For baking
$\frac{1}{4}$ cup dark brown sugar
$\frac{1}{4}$ teaspoon ground mace
grated rind and juice of 1 orange
1$\frac{1}{2}$ cups cider
watercress (for garnish)

Method
Allow $\frac{1}{2}$–1 lb of ham per person, depending on the amount of bone included. If the ham is heavily cured (like Virginia ham) immerse it for 4 hours in cold water and then drain. If lightly cured, cook it without soaking. Put the ham in a large saucepan with the vegetables, water to cover, bouquet garni and peppercorns. Cover and simmer gently 1$\frac{1}{4}$ hours for a 2 lb cut, or 30 minutes per lb for cuts over 3 lb (20 minutes per lb is enough for large hams over 10 lb).

When the ham is cooked, drain it and peel away the skin. This is easily done by carefully lifting corner of skin with a knife and pulling with the fingers. If the ham is very hot, hold skin with a cloth or paper towel. Set ham in a baking pan, fat side upwards.

Combine sugar, mace, orange rind and juice to form a paste; spread over ham and pour cider around it. Bake in a moderately hot oven (375°F) for 30 minutes or until golden, basting often.

Watchpoint: wait until the sugar begins to brown on the ham before basting with cider. You need to keep the ham moist, but it's not too difficult to baste the lean part of ham and avoid sugared crust.

Finish the top as follows: if using an electric stove, caramelize the sugar crust by placing under a hot broiler for 5–7 minutes until crisp and brown. If using a gas stove, heat two metal skewers in the flame until red hot. Take each skewer in turn and hold lightly on the sugar crust to burn decorative lines.

Arrange ham on a platter and if serving hot, let stand in a warm place 15 minutes before serving to make carving easier. If serving cold, allow ham to become completely cold before carving. Garnish with watercress and serve with raisin or Cumberland sauce.

Bouquet garni (a bunch of herbs) is traditionally made of 2–3 parsley stalks, a sprig of thyme and a bay leaf (tied together with string if used in liquids which are to be strained). Otherwise, herbs should be tied in a piece of cheesecloth for easy removal before serving the dish. If you have no fresh thyme use $\frac{1}{4}$ teaspoon dried thyme.

Accompaniments to Entrée

Raisin Sauce

$\frac{1}{2}$ cup raisins, cut or chopped into small pieces
1 cup sugar
$\frac{1}{2}$ cup water
1 tablespoon Worcestershire sauce
2 tablespoons butter
3 tablespoons wine vinegar
few drops Tabasco sauce
salt and pepper
pinch of ground mace
$\frac{1}{4}$ cup red currant jelly

Method
Dissolve sugar in water, then boil steadily for 5 minutes. Add remaining ingredients and simmer gently until the red currant jelly has dissolved. Serve hot or cold with ham.

Alternative sauce

Cumberland Sauce

$\frac{1}{2}$ cup red currant jelly
juice of 1 orange
juice of $\frac{1}{2}$ lemon
$\frac{1}{4}$ cup port

Method
Gently heat red currant jelly until melted and stir in strained orange juice with lemon juice and port. Serve hot or cold.

If this sauce is not to be followed by oranges in caramel, needle-like strips of orange peel may be added to the sauce. The strips should first be blanched in boiling water for 5 minutes.

Mashed Potatoes

4 medium potatoes, peeled
3–4 tablespoons butter
salt and pepper
$\frac{1}{2}$ cup milk, scalded

To prepare mashed potatoes early and keep hot, cook them as follows.

Method
Cut potatoes into even-sized pieces (if very large), and cook in boiling salted water for 15–20 minutes or until tender. Test with the point of a fine knife or trussing needle. Do not use the thick prongs of a fork or the potato will break.

Watchpoint: take care to keep potatoes covered with water so they cook evenly.

When the potatoes are tender, tilt lid of pan and pour away the water. Return to a low heat and, with lid half-closed, continue cooking a few minutes until potatoes are dry. Then add butter – as much as you like – and mash potatoes with a potato masher or fork. Season to taste. If not serving at once, press potatoes firmly to bottom of saucepan and pour on the scalded milk. Do not stir, but replace lid and keep pan in a warm place until ready to serve. Keep hot in this way for up to 30 minutes; the potatoes will absorb the milk on standing. Just before serving, beat potatoes well with a wooden spoon or small electric beater until fluffy, adding more milk if necessary.

Dessert

Oranges in Caramel

8 large seedless oranges (navel are best)
1 cup sugar
$\frac{1}{2}$ cup water
$\frac{1}{2}$ cup warm water

8 wooden toothpicks

Method
In a heavy-based pan, dissolve the sugar in $\frac{1}{2}$ cup water over gentle heat.
Watchpoint: the rule for boiling sugar is to dissolve sugar slowly, then boil steadily to prevent crystalizing. Keep pan on a very low heat as the water should not boil until every grain of sugar has dissolved. Do not stir. The sugar can be moved from the base of the pan by drawing a spoon carefully through it.

When all the sugar has dissolved, bring to a boil and cook steadily to a rich brown caramel – it will change color quickly towards the end of cooking. Remove from the heat and hold pan over a bowl of warm water so that the base just touches the water (to prevent further cooking). Cover the hand holding the saucepan with a cloth (the mixture may splash and scald) and quickly pour in $\frac{1}{2}$ cup warm water. Return to the heat and bring mixture just back to a boil to dissolve the caramel; pour into a bowl and cool.

Using a potato peeler, thinly pare the peel from 1 orange, cut it into needle-like strips, cook 5 minutes in boiling water, drain and dry on paper towels.

Cut peel, pith and outer membrane from oranges, leaving flesh exposed. This is best done with a serrated-edge knife and, if you cut with a sawing action, you should not lose much juice. On a plate to catch juice, slice each orange across the segments. Reshape orange by spearing segments together with a toothpick and arrange in a deep glass dish. Pour caramel on top, sprinkle orange peel on top and chill.

Above: use a serrated-edge knife with a sawing action to remove orange peel and pith. Below: after slicing oranges, reshape and secure the slices in place with a toothpick

Accompaniment to Dessert

Brandy Snaps

$\frac{1}{2}$ cup butter
$\frac{1}{2}$ cup sugar
$\frac{1}{3}$ cup dark molasses
$\frac{1}{2}$ cup flour
pinch of salt
1 teaspoon ground ginger
1 teaspoon lemon juice
$\frac{1}{2}$ teaspoon vanilla

Makes about 20 brandy snaps; 1 cup heavy cream, whipped, should fill 20.

Method
Set oven at moderately low (325°F). In a saucepan melt butter, sugar and molasses, stirring until butter is dissolved. Cool slightly. Sift flour with salt and ginger into the mixture, and stir well, adding lemon juice and vanilla.

Drop the mixture a teaspoon at a time at least 4 inches apart on a well-greased baking sheet. Bake in heated oven for 7–8 minutes or until brown. Remove cookies from sheet with a sharp knife, turn over and roll around the handle of a wooden spoon. If they cool before all are rolled, return to the oven for a few moments. Store cooled brandy snaps in an airtight tin and, just before serving, fill with whipped cream, preferably piping the cream through a pastry bag fitted with a star tube (see page 24).

Above: when baking brandy snaps, use only one teaspoon of the mixture and leave space for expansion between each of the spoonsful.
Below: before brandy snaps are cool, roll them around the handle of a wooden spoon

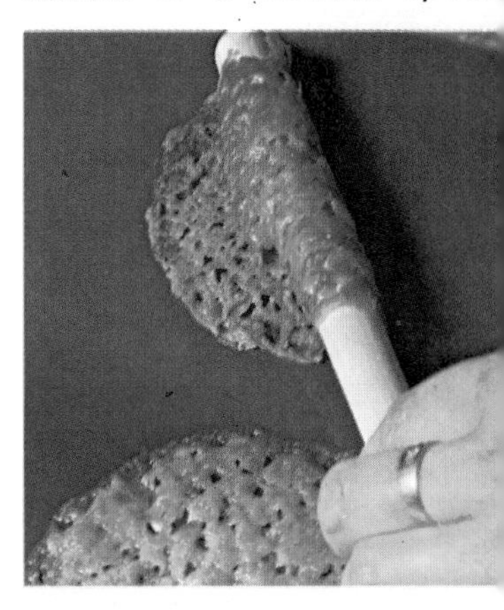

Below: just before serving, fill brandy snaps with cream

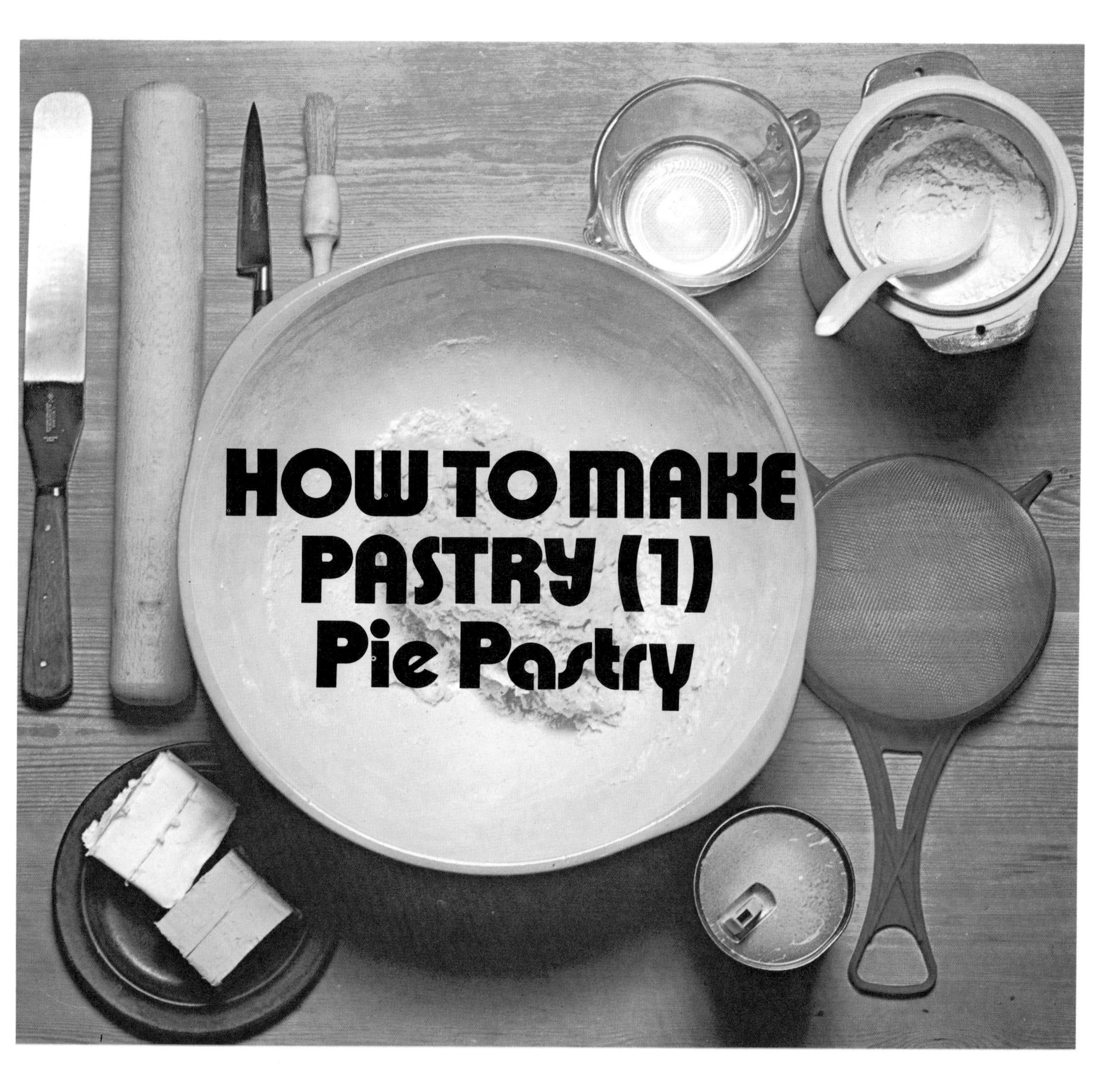
HOW TO MAKE
PASTRY (1)
Pie Pastry

Pie Pastry

Pastry is used in so many dishes that it is one of the first skills a cook must master. Pastry-making is not difficult if you follow certain rules:

1 Work in a cool, airy room. Plan to make pastry before the kitchen becomes warm from other cooking as a warm, damp atmosphere gives unsatisfactory results.

2 Use all-purpose flour and sift it after measuring. Use firm but not hard fat (which would not blend properly with the flour) and ice-cold water for mixing.

3 Handle flour and fat lightly. When rubbing fat into flour, keep lifting it up and crumbling the mixture between your fingers. This movement helps to aerate the dough. Shake the bowl after 1–2 minutes to bring the larger lumps of fat to the surface and to show you how much more rubbing-in is necessary. This is especially helpful when making rich pie pastry as over-rubbing makes the pastry greasy.

4 Be sure that the correct amount of water is added. This will vary slightly with the quality and type of flour as well as how long it has been stored. Too dry a mixture makes the dough hard to handle; it cracks when rolled out, crumbles after baking and will be dry to eat. Too wet a dough shrinks and loses shape while baking, and also results in tough, hard pastry. The amount of water is usually given in a recipe, and it is important to add at least two-thirds of the given quantity to the dry ingredients before mixing begins. This avoids over-working and brings the ingredients quickly to a firm, smooth dough, especially when making the foundation dough for puff pastry.

5 A marble slab is ideal for rolling out pastry dough because it is smooth, solid and cool; otherwise use a Formica-type surface or keep a board especially for this purpose. Once dough has been rolled out, always scrape the board thoroughly before rolling out new dough to remove any that may have stuck and which might cause further sticking. (This applies particularly to flaky or puff pastry when rolling is of paramount importance.) Use a minimum amount of flour for sprinkling when rolling, otherwise too much will go into the pastry and spoil it. A heavy, plain wooden rolling pin without handles is best, especially for puff pastry.

6 Chill completed pastry dough for about 30 minutes; this removes any elasticity, which might cause shrinkage, and gives the dough a chance to 'relax'.

7 When baking pastry, it is essential to preheat oven to the required temperature. The immediate heat 'sets' pastry in its correct shape, making it possible to control the exact length of cooking.

Basic Proportions

The basic proportions of ingredients for regular pie pastry are $\frac{1}{4}$ teaspoon salt to every cup of flour, and 1 part fat to 3 parts flour. The more fat added to pastry, the shorter (i.e. lighter and crisper) it will be; such a rich mixture is best for pies that will be eaten cold. Butter, margarine, lard or shortening may be used, and a mixture of fats gives the best results, e.g. butter and shortening because butter gives a good flavor and shortening a light texture. For rich pie pastry, allow 1 egg yolk to every 2 cups flour.

Quantity Terms

Terms like '1 cup quantity of pastry' refer to the amount obtained by using 1 cup flour, NOT 1 cup prepared dough. As a guide, 2 cup quantity of pastry will line two 9 inch pie pans or is enough for one 9 inch double crust pie.

For pie pastry, when the pieces of fat are well coated with flour, rub in with the fingertips until the mixture looks like fine crumbs

Pie Pastry

2 cups flour
$\frac{1}{2}$ teaspoon salt
$\frac{2}{3}$ cup butter, margarine, lard, or shortening, or a mixture of butter or margarine with shortening
4–5 tablespoons cold water

Method

Sift flour with salt into a bowl. Cut in fat with a pastry blender or two round-bladed knives, using one in each hand. As soon as the pieces of fat are well coated with flour, rub in with fingertips until the mixture looks like fine crumbs.

Make a well in the center, pour in 4 tablespoons water and mix quickly with a knife. Press together with fingers and add more water if necessary to give a firm, not sticky, dough.

Turn onto a floured board or marble slab and knead dough lightly for a few seconds until smooth. Wrap in wax paper, plastic wrap or a plastic bag and chill 30 minutes before using.

Rich Pie Pastry

2 cups flour
$\frac{1}{2}$ teaspoon salt
$\frac{2}{3}$ cup butter
2 teaspoons sugar (for sweet pastry) – optional
1 egg yolk
3–4 tablespoons cold water

Method

Sift flour with salt into a bowl. Cut butter into flour until in small pieces and well coated, then rub in with the fingertips until mixture looks like crumbs. Make a well in the center and add sugar, egg yolk, and 3 tablespoons water and stir to combine. Draw flour into mixture in the center quickly with a knife. Press together with fingers, adding more water if necessary to form a smooth dough.

Turn onto a floured board or marble slab and knead lightly for a few seconds until smooth. Wrap in wax paper, plastic wrap or a plastic bag. Chill 30 minutes before using.

For even richer pie pastry, see the recipe for Bavarian apple slice on page 52.

Pastry Finishes

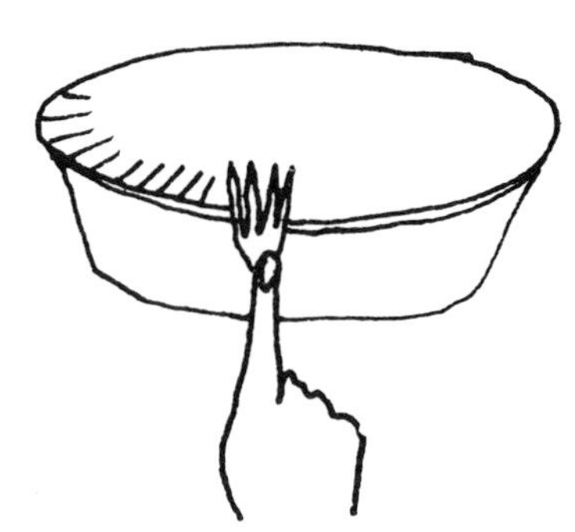

1 When using only one layer of pastry, **forking** the edge is adequate. Press the back of the fork prongs into the pastry edge

2 When using two layers, **seal** the edges by placing the side of the left forefinger on top of the pastry edge and, with the back of a broad-bladed knife, make indentations in double edges to seal. This prevents the layers from splitting when baked

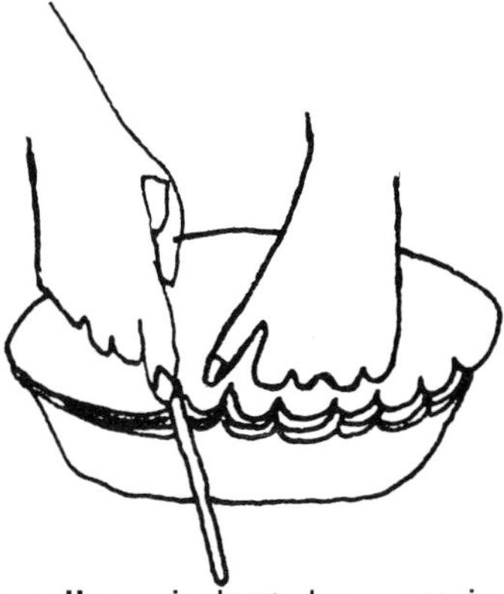

3 To **scallop**, indent by pressing the left thumb on top of the outer edge. Draw the back of the knife towards the center for $\frac{1}{2}$ inch, repeating all the way around. Leave $\frac{3}{4}$ inch between cuts for savory pies; $\frac{1}{4}$ inch for sweet ones

4 Crimp by pinching the pastry edge between thumb and forefinger of each hand, twisting slightly in opposite directions

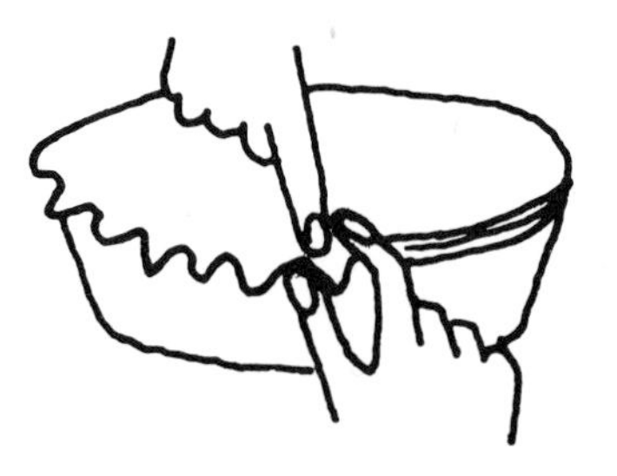

5 Flute by placing a forefinger on the pastry edge, then pinching the pastry with the forefinger and thumb of the other hand. Repeat all around the pie at $\frac{1}{2}$ inch intervals

Dessert Pies

A slice of apple pie with slits in the pastry crust to allow air to escape during cooking

Dessert Pies

A pie means different things to different people. Here in the U.S. a pie has a crust underneath and may or may not have one on top as well. In England, a crust always covers the top of a pie (and it is often made in a deep dish), and a single crust underneath indicates a tart. Some tart and tartlet recipes are included here. The original definition of tart comes from France, where an open pastry shell that is filled with a variety of sweet or savory mixtures is called a 'tarte'.

For a professional touch, follow the pastry finishes shown on page 50 when you are making pie recipes.

American Apple Pie

2 cup quantity of pie pastry

For filling
5–6 tart apples
½–⅔ cup brown, or white, sugar
1 tablespoon cornstarch
½ teaspoon cinnamon
¼ teaspoon nutmeg
1 tablespoon lemon juice
1 tablespoon butter
sugar (for glazing)
ice cream, or heavy cream (to serve – optional)

9 inch pie pan

Method

Make pastry and chill. Peel, core and slice apples into a bowl and stir in sugar, cornstarch, cinnamon and nutmeg until apple slices are well coated. Divide pastry and roll half into a circle to line pie pan. Fill pie with apple mixture, leveling the top, sprinkle with lemon juice and dot with butter. Roll out the remaining pastry to cover the pie; seal and decorate edges. Brush the top with water and sprinkle with sugar to glaze. Bake in a hot oven (425°F) for 10 minutes, reduce heat to moderate (350°F) and then continue baking 40 minutes or until the crust is brown and apples are tender. Serve hot or cold with ice cream or heavy cream.

English Apple Pie

1½ cup quantity of pie pastry

For filling
4–5 tart apples, or mildly acid dessert apples
strip of lemon rind
4–6 tablespoons brown, or white, sugar
little grated lemon rind, or 1–2 whole cloves (optional)

Deep 8 inch pie pan

This is one of the oldest of English dishes and delicious when properly made. Traditionally, it is baked in a deep oval English pie dish, but any deep pie pan will do. Use an apple which holds its shape when cooked, like Granny Smith's, or a sharp dessert apple such as Jonathan's.

Method

Peel, quarter and core apples and keep them covered in a bowl. Put cores and peel in a saucepan with strip of lemon rind; barely cover with water and simmer 15–20 minutes.

Prepare pastry and chill. Fill pie pan with apple slices, cutting each quarter into 2–3 pieces, and layering them with sugar (vary the amount according to the acidity of the fruit), and lemon rind or cloves.

Watchpoint: do not slice the apples too thinly or the juice will run quickly and may make the slices tough and tasteless.

Dome the fruit slightly above the edge of the pan (this will prevent the pastry from falling in), and pour in enough strained apple juice to half fill the pan. (Water may be used instead of juice but, for maximum flavor, the juice is preferable.)

Roll pastry ¼ inch thick, cut 1–2 strips from the sides and lay these on the dampened edge of the pie pan. Press down and brush them with cold water. Lift up remaining pastry by rolling it around rolling pin and lay it on the pie, pressing down the edge. Then lift the pan in one hand and cut away excess pastry, holding knife slantwise towards bottom of pan to obtain a slightly overhanging edge. Crimp or flute edge with the fingers, brush pastry lightly with water, scatter with sugar (for a dry glaze), or leave plain and sprinkle with sugar after baking.

Set pan on a baking sheet for ease of taking in and out of the oven and to catch any juice that might spill over. Bake in a moderately hot oven (375°F) for 25 minutes or until pastry is brown. Turn down heat to moderate (350°F) and cook for 10 minutes more or until apples are soft.

Bavarian Apple Slice

For rich pie pastry
1½ cups flour
¼ teaspoon salt
½ cup butter
3 tablespoons sugar
1 egg yolk
1½–2 tablespoons milk

For apple mixture
3–4 tart apples
2 tablespoons seedless raisins
2 tablespoons golden raisins
3 tablespoons fresh white breadcrumbs
1–2 tablespoons brown, or white, sugar
1 teaspoon ground cinnamon
confectioners' sugar (for sprinkling)
1 cup sour, or ½ cup heavy cream, stiffly whipped (to serve)

Method

Rub butter lightly into sifted flour and salt in a bowl; add sugar. Mix egg yolk with milk and stir into pastry to bind together. Chill 30 minutes. Peel, core and slice apples, put them in a bowl with raisins, crumbs, sugar and cinnamon and mix well.

Knead pastry lightly until smooth, and roll thinly to a rectangle about 6 X 12 inches. Lift onto a baking sheet (it should have no edges so the slice can be moved easily after cooking) and trim pastry edges. Pile apple mixture in the center, leaving 1–1½ inches of pastry on each side. Lift these sides up and over mixture with a palette knife so they rest on the mixture, but leave a gap in the middle to show the filling. Press pastry down lightly with a knife so the sides remain in place during baking.

Bake in a moderately hot oven (375°F) for 35 minutes or until pastry is lightly brown and apples are cooked. Slide onto a wire rack to cool, then sprinkle generously with confectioners' sugar before cutting into slices for serving. Serve with sour, or whipped, cream.

Yorkshire Apple Cake

For pie pastry
1½ cups flour
¼ teaspoon salt
5 tablespoons butter
3 tablespoons lard, or shortening
2 tablespoons cold water

For filling
4–5 tart apples
1 tablespoon butter
strip of lemon rind and juice of ½ lemon
2 tablespoons thick honey, or 3–4 tablespoons sugar

Shallow 8 inch pie pan

Method

Make pastry and chill.

Rub a shallow saucepan with butter. Peel, core and slice (not too thinly) the apples, and put into saucepan with the remaining ingredients. Cover and cook gently until juice begins to run, then remove lid and cook quickly to a thick pulp, stirring frequently. Turn onto a plate to cool. Roll out a little less than half the pastry to a circle and line the shallow pie pan, pressing down and trimming the edge. Add apple mixture, leaving an inch of pastry edge exposed and moisten this with water. Roll out remaining pastry, keeping it thicker than the bottom layer, and lay over the plate. Press edges firmly together and crimp or mark them with a fork. Leave plain or brush with water and sprinkle with sugar before baking. Place on a hot baking sheet and bake in a moderately hot oven (375°F) for 40 minutes or until pastry is brown and crisp. Serve the cake hot with heavy cream, or cold with a wedge of Cheddar cheese.

Coffee Almond Pie

1½ cup quantity of rich pie pastry

For filling
2 tablespoons dry instant coffee
1 cup boiling water
¼ cup light brown sugar
¾ cup milk
1 tablespoon flour
2 tablespoons cornstarch
2 egg yolks, beaten
¼ cup butter

For topping
1 tablespoon sugar
2 teaspoons rum
¾ cup heavy cream, whipped until it holds a soft shape
½ cup shredded almonds

9 inch loose-based pie pan; pastry bag; star tube

Method

Make pastry dough and chill. Line pie pan and bake blind (see box on page 55).

To make filling: pour the boiling water onto the coffee and sugar and stir until dissolved. In a saucepan stir the milk into the flour and cornstarch until smooth. Add coffee mixture and bring to a boil, stirring constantly. Cook 1 minute or until clear and thickened. Stir a little of the hot mixture into the beaten egg yolks, add this to the remaining mixture in the pan and cook 1 minute longer. Take pan from the heat and beat in the butter, a small piece at a time. Pour the coffee mixture into the pastry shell and chill.

To make topping: stir the sugar and rum into the lightly whipped cream and continue beating until stiff. Fill the cream into the pastry bag fitted with a star tube and decorate the top of the pie with a lattice. Pipe rosettes of cream around the edge and sprinkle the browned almonds on top.

To Brown Whole Almonds

Blanch and remove skins and bake 8–10 minutes in a moderately hot oven (375°F) or until browned.

Butterscotch Cream Pie

1½ cup quantity of rich pie pastry

For filling
¼ cup butter
½ cup dark brown sugar
½ cup boiling water
2 tablespoons cornstarch
1 tablespoon flour
large pinch of salt
1¼ cups milk
2 egg yolks, slightly beaten
½ teaspoon vanilla

To decorate
¾ cup heavy cream, stiffly whipped
2 tablespoons slivered almonds, browned and finely chopped

8 inch pie pan

Method

Make pastry dough and chill. Line pie pan and bake blind (see box on page 55).

In a heavy pan, melt butter and cook until golden. Stir in sugar and, when foaming, boil 2–3 minutes. Take from heat and stir in boiling water.

In a saucepan, combine cornstarch, flour, salt and mix to a smooth paste with milk. Stir in brown sugar mixture and cook over gentle heat, stirring, until boiling and thickened. Cook 1 minute, pour half the mixture into egg yolks, stir and return to remaining mixture in pan. Cook 1 minute longer, stirring until the mixture thickens slightly, take from heat and add vanilla. Cool, pour into baked pie shell and chill until set. Just before serving, top with whipped cream and sprinkle with almonds.

Tartlet cases filled with ripe and juicy strawberries will tempt any sweet tooth

Fruit Tartlets

These can be made with a wide variety of fruit: blueberries, raspberries, peeled and halved small fresh peaches, skinned and seeded grapes, pitted cherries, etc., and a selection of tartlets containing different colored fruits looks particularly attractive on a platter. Follow the method for strawberry tartlets, using a red currant glaze for red and purple fruits and an apricot jam glaze for green and yellow fruits.

Strawberry Tartlets

For rich pie pastry
$1\frac{1}{4}$ cups flour
$\frac{1}{4}$ teaspoon salt
6 tablespoons butter
1 teaspoon sugar
1 egg yolk
$1\frac{1}{2}$–2 tablespoons cold water

For filling
1 pint hulled strawberries
$\frac{1}{2}$ cup red currant jelly (for glaze)

Small tartlet pans

Method

Make pastry dough and chill. Roll out thinly and, using a cookie cutter that is $\frac{1}{2}$ inch larger than the tartlet pans, cut circles from pastry. Press these into the pans, chill and bake blind (see box). Cool shells and remove the pans. Brush all the shells with red currant glaze, fill with strawberries and brush generously again with glaze – it should fill in any cracks and hold strawberries firmly in place. Serve within 3–4 hours.

Thickened Fruit Juice Glaze

This is made from the juice of cooked or canned fruit, and is usually used to glaze the fruit itself. For each cup of juice, allow 1 teaspoon arrowroot or cornstarch (arrowroot has a less sticky consistency) and mix it with 1 tablespoon of juice to a smooth paste. In a saucepan bring remaining juice to a boil with 1 tablespoon red or yellow jam, whichever is appropriate to the fruit. Take from heat and stir in the arrowroot mixture. Return to heat and bring just to a boil, stirring. Remove arrowroot from heat at once; if using cornstarch, continue cooking 1 minute. Strain and use glaze warm.

Apricot Jam Glaze

For use with all yellow and green fruit. The glaze keeps well, so make 2 cups or more at a time to use as needed. Store in a covered jar.

In a saucepan bring slowly to a boil 12 oz of apricot jam with the juice of $\frac{1}{2}$ lemon and 2 tablespoons water. Stir until smooth, simmer 5 minutes, strain and return to the pan. Boil 5 minutes more and pour into a jar for storage. To use, melt and continue boiling until thick, then brush generously over the fruit. If using a smooth jam or jelly with no pieces of fruit, do not add water.

Red Currant Jelly Glaze

For use with all red and purple fruit as it enhances color.

Beat jelly with a fork or small whisk until it softens, then rub through a strainer into a small saucepan. Heat gently without stirring until quite clear (boiling spoils the color and flavor). When brushing over the fruit, always use a very soft brush and work from the center out, drawing the brush, well laden with glaze, towards the edge.

To Bake Blind

To prevent shrinkage – the sides from falling in and the bottom rising – when an unfilled pie or tartlet shell is baking, the pastry dough must be lined with foil and filled with rice or dried beans. First chill pastry thoroughly, then line it with foil, pressing well into the corners and against the sides. Fill center three-quarters full with rice or dried beans (these can be used again and again for the same purpose).

Bake in a preheated hot oven (400° F) until pastry is golden brown, allowing 10–12 minutes for small tartlets. For a pie shell, turn down heat to moderately hot (375° F) after 10 minutes and continue cooking about 15 minutes longer. For both tartlets and pies, remove the foil halfway through cooking, or when pastry has set firmly, to allow it to become crisp and brown.

Coconut Cream Pie

$1\frac{1}{2}$ cup quantity of rich pie pastry

For filling
$\frac{3}{4}$ cup shredded coconut
2 tablespoons rum
3 egg yolks
$\frac{1}{2}$ cup sugar
1 tablespoon cornstarch
$\frac{1}{2}$ cup milk
1 tablespoon butter

For topping
3 egg whites
$\frac{1}{3}$ cup sugar
$\frac{1}{2}$ cup shredded coconut (optional)

8 inch pie pan

Method

Make pastry dough and chill. Line pie pan and bake blind (see box, left).

To make filling: beat egg yolks and sugar until thick and light; stir in cornstarch. Scald milk, stir a little into egg yolk mixture and add this to remaining milk. Bring mixture to a boil, stirring constantly, and cook 1 minute until thick and shiny. Stir in coconut and cook 1 minute longer. Take pan from heat, beat in butter, a small piece at a time, and stir in rum. Pour filling into pie shell and let cool.

To make meringue: beat egg whites until they hold a stiff peak. Beat in 2 tablespoons sugar until glossy and fold in the remaining sugar with a metal spoon.

Pile meringue on filling, sealing it to pastry to avoid shrinkage. Bake in a hot oven (400°F) for 8–10 minutes or until lightly browned. Cool. If adding coconut, spread on a baking sheet, and bake in heated oven for 10 minutes or until golden. Sprinkle on pie.

Coconut cream pie is topped with meringue and sprinkled with browned shredded coconut (recipe is on page 55)

Meringue is piled on top of the filled pastry shell for lemon meringue pie (recipe is on page 58)

Lemon Meringue Pie

For rich pie pastry
$1\frac{1}{2}$ cups flour
$\frac{1}{4}$ teaspoon salt
7 tablespoons butter
1 egg yolk
1–2 tablespoons cold water

For filling
$\frac{3}{4}$ cup sugar
$\frac{1}{4}$ teaspoon salt
1 cup water
3 tablespoons cornstarch
2 egg yolks
$\frac{1}{4}$ cup lemon juice
2 tablespoons butter
1 teaspoon grated lemon rind

For meringue
2 egg whites
6 tablespoons sugar

8 inch pie pan

Method

Make pastry dough and chill. Line pie pan and bake blind (see box on page 55).

Dissolve sugar with salt in $\frac{3}{4}$ cup of the water in a saucepan over heat, then bring to a boil. Mix cornstarch with remaining water to a smooth paste, take sugar syrup from heat and stir in cornstarch. Return to heat and cook, stirring constantly, until thick and clear. Take from heat. Beat egg yolks with lemon juice until slightly thick, stir into cornstarch mixture and bring just back to a boil. Take from heat, stir in butter and lemon rind, cool slightly and pour into pastry shell. Cool.

To make meringue: beat egg whites until they hold a stiff peak and then beat in 2 tablespoons sugar until mixture is glossy. Fold in remaining sugar with a metal spoon. **Watchpoint**: whisking in this small quantity of sugar helps to set the whites; the remaining sugar is folded in to retain the air already beaten into the whites. If you overbeat, the sugar starts to liquefy and the egg whites collapse, resulting in a thin layer of meringue that is tough on top.

Pile meringue on filling to cover it completely, seal it to pastry to avoid shrinkage and sprinkle with sugar. To set rather than cook the meringue, place in a low oven (275° F) for 15 minutes or until lightly browned. The consistency should be that of a marshmallow – firm to cut, yet soft with a crisp coating.

Chocolate Meringue Pie

$1\frac{1}{2}$ cup quantity of rich pie pastry

For filling
$\frac{1}{4}$ cup cocoa
$\frac{1}{2}$ cup sugar
pinch of salt
2 tablespoons cornstarch
2 cups milk
2 egg yolks, slightly beaten
2 tablespoons butter
$\frac{1}{2}$ teaspoon vanilla

For meringue
2 egg whites
6 tablespoons sugar

8 inch pie pan

Method

Make pastry dough and chill. Line pie pan and bake blind (see box on page 55).

In a saucepan mix cocoa, sugar, salt and cornstarch to a smooth paste with milk. Stir over gentle heat until boiling and thickened and cook 1 minute. Blend half the mixture into egg yolks, return to remaining mixture in pan and cook 1 minute longer or until slightly thickened, stirring constantly. Beat in butter and vanilla, cool slightly and pour into baked pie shell.

To make meringue: beat egg whites until they hold a stiff peak. Beat in 2 tablespoons sugar until glossy and fold in remaining sugar with a metal spoon. Pile meringue on filling, sealing it to pastry to avoid shrinkage. Sprinkle it with sugar and bake in a low oven (275° F) for 15 minutes or until meringue is lightly browned.

Baked Graham Cracker Crust

$1\frac{1}{3}$ cups graham cracker crumbs
$\frac{1}{4}$ cup sugar
$\frac{1}{4}$ cup softened butter

9 inch loose-based pie pan

Method

In a bowl combine ingredients and blend until crumbly. Press evenly over bottom and sides of pie pan. Bake shell in moderately hot oven (375°F) for 8 minutes or until edges are lightly browned.

Lemon Chiffon Pie

9 inch baked graham cracker crust

For filling
$\frac{1}{2}$ envelope gelatin
2 tablespoons cold water
2 eggs, separated
$\frac{1}{2}$ cup sugar
pinch of salt
juice of 1 lemon and grated peel of $\frac{1}{2}$ lemon
$\frac{1}{2}$ cup heavy cream, whipped until it holds a soft shape

Method

Make pie shell and cool. In a small saucepan, sprinkle gelatin over cold water and let stand 5 minutes or until spongy. Meanwhile beat egg yolks with half the sugar, the salt, lemon juice and peel until light and creamy. Pour into the top of a double boiler and cook, stirring, over gentle heat until mixture is the consistency of heavy cream. Take from heat. Dissolve gelatin over a pan of hot water and stir into lemon mixture. Cool, stirring occasionally. Beat egg whites until they hold a stiff peak and beat in remaining sugar a spoonful at a time until this meringue is smooth and glossy.

When lemon mixture starts to set, beat until smooth and fold into meringue with the whipped cream.

Pour into pie shell and chill until set. Take from refrigerator 20 minutes before serving.

Pie Pastry

Lemon chiffon pie – baked graham cracker crust is filled with a lemon and cream mixture and set with gelatin

HOW TO BOIL & STEAM

Boiling is the plainest and most economical method of cooking and also develops the natural flavor of the food. The term 'boiling' means that food is immersed and cooked in water, and vegetables and seasonings are often added to meat cooked in this way to give extra flavor.

There are two methods of boiling meat:

1 A cut like brisket of beef is plunged into boiling salted water and boiled for 5 minutes to firm the outside and seal in the juices. The heat is then reduced and meat simmered until tender. Place meat in a pan, with side that is to be uppermost when served on the bottom. Skim often during cooking and allow 20–25 minutes cooking time per pound plus 20–25 minutes over.

2 Meat for soups and stocks is covered with cold water and salt added, then left to stand for up to 20 minutes before cooking. This allows the cold water and salt to draw out the juices of the meat. The length of cooking time depends, as in the previous method, on the weight of meat and only gentle heat should be used. To transfer maximum flavor to liquid, cut the meat into small pieces.

Note: put salted meats into tepid water with no salt added so they won't be too salty.

To steam is to cook by moist heat, a comparatively slow method as the food does not come into direct contact with boiling water – only with its vapor. Steaming food takes half as long again as boiling and twice as long if the texture of the food is particularly dense.

There are two ways to steam:

1 Using a steamer – a container with perforations at the bottom and a close-fitting lid. Some steamers have graduated ridges at the base rim so they will fit snugly onto saucepans of varying sizes. For a perfect fit, saucepans can be bought complete with matching steamers. The food is placed directly in the top half – the steamer – and therefore is in immediate contact with the steam. This method is used for vegetables like corn, squash and potatoes, for puddings, and for fish and poultry. Different foods wrapped separately in foil can be cooked together in one steamer.

2 Using two plates. The food is put between two heatproof plates over a pan of boiling water and cooks in its own juice and steam. The food will be delicate in flavor and easily digested – an ideal way to cook for children or invalids.

Boiling & Steaming

Boiling is an excellent method of cooking a large, old chicken. Serve with parsley sauce (recipe is on page 62)

BOILING

Boiled Chicken with Parsley Sauce

5 lb fowl, or roasting chicken
1 large carrot, quartered
1 large onion, quartered
2 stalks of celery (optional)
bouquet garni
6 peppercorns
½ teaspoon salt
cold water
¼ lb sliced bacon (for garnish)

For parsley sauce
1 large bunch of fresh parsley
2 cups milk
1 bay leaf
1 blade of mace or ¼ teaspoon ground mace
6 peppercorns
3 tablespoons butter
3 tablespoons flour
salt and pepper

This recipe is an excellent example of the first method of boiling. Serves 6 people.

Method

Set the bird on its back in a large saucepan. Surround it with vegetables, bouquet garni, peppercorns and salt. For a fowl, pour in enough water barely to cover; for a roasting chicken, add enough just to cover the thighs. Put lid on pan and bring slowly to a boil. Simmer fowl 2 hours and roasting chicken 1¼ hours or until tender and no pink juice runs out when thigh is pierced with a fork. Turn bird over from time to time. When cooked allow to cool slightly in the pan.

To prepare sauce, remove parsley sprigs from stalks, reserving them, and wash well. Boil sprigs for 7 minutes in salted water, drain, squeeze dry and rub through a strainer to make 1 tablespoon parsley purée.

Infuse milk by heating it almost to boiling and keeping hot for 7 minutes with bay leaf, mace, peppercorns and parsley stalks; then strain it. Melt butter, and, when foaming, remove from heat and stir in the flour. Pour on milk and bring to a boil, stirring until sauce thickens. Simmer 2 minutes, add parsley purée and season. Keep warm. Cook bacon until crisp and drain it on paper towel.

Drain chicken, carve (discarding the skin from fowl), and arrange on a platter. Spoon over some of the sauce, serving the rest separately, and garnish the dish with bacon. Serve with boiled rice or mashed potatoes.

Pot-au-feu

3 lb short rib, or plate of beef, rolled with the bones
1 lb veal bones
2 teaspoons salt
about 3 quarts water
2 large carrots, quartered
2–3 onions, one stuck with a clove
2–3 sticks of celery
4–6 small turnips
large bouquet garni

When doubling this recipe, about 6 lb of meat is needed; choose another cut as well as the ribs, e.g. 2–3 lb brisket, chuck or rump, thus combining lean meat with fat.

This recipe is an example of the second method of boiling.

The soup, which is the liquid in which the meat was cooked, can precede the boiled beef entrée or it can be left to simmer for another hour to concentrate the flavor. Fresh root vegetables can be added to the broth while it is reducing. They are sliced or diced, when cooked, to be served in the soup bowl with slices of French bread that have been covered with fat from the soup and baked separately.

Method

Put meat in a large kettle with salted water and the washed beef and veal bones. Stand 20 minutes. Put on a low heat, uncovered, and bring to a boil. As scum rises to the surface, skim it with a slotted metal spoon and, as liquid reaches simmering point, add ¼ cup cold water. Bring to a boil again, skim once more and add a further ¼ cup cold water. If liquid is still not clear, repeat process once more. This not only helps to clear the liquid, which will become soup, but also removes any strong flavor of bone. Simmer 30–40 minutes, then add vegetables and bouquet garni. Skim again if necessary, and partially cover pan with lid. Simmer until meat is tender (2½–3 hours). Then remove meat and serve with the vegetables.

Return pan to heat and continue to simmer broth, uncovered, until strong and well flavored. If served as soup, add coarsely chopped cooked vegetables 10 minutes before the end of reduction. Skim off fat and spread it on slices of French bread. Bake slices in the oven until hot and crisp and place in soup bowls. Pour over hot soup with vegetables and serve.

Austrian Boiled Beef with Horseradish Sauce

3 lb boneless beef rump, bottom round or brisket, rolled
2 quarts cold water
salt
1 onion, stuck with 3 cloves
4 medium carrots, quartered
3 stalks of celery, sliced
1 medium turnip, quartered
1 leek, washed and quartered (optional)
bouquet garni
6 peppercorns

For horseradish sauce
2 tablespoons freshly grated horseradish
2 tablespoons butter
1 medium onion, finely chopped
2 tablespoons flour
1 cup beef stock
juice of ½ lemon
pepper
sugar (to taste)
3 tablespoons heavy cream

Method

In a large pan place beef in the water with 1 teaspoon salt. Stand 15 minutes, then bring slowly to a boil, skimming frequently.

Add onion, carrot, celery, turnip, leek, bouquet garni and peppercorns, cover pan, lower heat and simmer 2–2½ hours or until meat is very tender when pierced with a fork.

Drain the beef, arrange on a serving platter and keep warm. Strain the stock, pressing vegetables to extract the juice, and skim off any fat. Taste stock for seasoning and serve as a soup before the beef if you like, reserving 1 cup to make the horseradish sauce.

For sauce: melt butter in a

saucepan and sauté the onion over medium heat until soft. Stir in flour and cook, stirring, until flour and onion are lightly browned. Add the stock, horseradish and lemon juice with salt, pepper and sugar to taste. Bring the sauce to a boil, stirring; simmer 3 minutes, take from heat and stir in the cream.

Serve the beef with boiled potatoes, and the horseradish sauce separately.

New England Boiled Dinner

3–4 lb corned beef
6 carrots, quartered
6 medium potatoes, quartered
1 medium yellow turnip, quartered
1 small green cabbage, quartered
1 lb crookneck, or butternut, squash, peeled and cut in thick slices
salt and pepper

Method

Place beef in a large kettle, cover with tepid water and a lid and bring slowly to a boil. Skim, then simmer gently for 2–3 hours or until meat is tender; 35 minutes before end of cooking, add carrots, potatoes and turnip. Then 15 minutes before end of cooking, add cabbage and squash. When adding vegetables, turn up the heat to bring liquid quickly back to a boil and reduce it again so simmering continues. At this stage, taste the liquid to see if seasoning is needed to flavor the vegetables. To serve, drain beef and arrange on a platter, surrounded by vegetables.

STEAMING

Cooking vegetables well is probably one of the most underrated skills in the kitchen. Often vegetables are served without any attempt having been made to ensure that all the flavor in them was retained during the cooking process.

Vegetables should never be overcooked – they should be just tender. The briefer the cooking time, the more the flavor will be retained and less will be lost to the cooking water. Steaming is one of the best ways to cook vegetables, and there are several types of steamer available.

Asparagus with Melted Butter

2 lb fresh asparagus
$\frac{1}{2}$ cup butter

Method

Trim hard bottom stalks of the asparagus. To be sure all stalks are the same length, cut them while still tied in a bunch. After untying them, rinse well in cold water and scrape lower part of stems thoroughly with a vegetable peeler to remove outer skin. Tie asparagus in several bunches and leave cut stems standing in a bowl of cold water until ready to cook.

Stand asparagus bunches, stems down, in 1–2 inches boiling salted water (in an asparagus cooker or tall pan). Cover and simmer 8–10 minutes or until upper stems are just tender. Lift bunches carefully from pan, drain on paper towels and arrange on a folded white napkin on a hot platter. Cut and remove the string from each bunch.

Melt butter gently in a small pan, but do not let it get too hot and oily. Skim well, pour into a hot sauce boat to serve.

Special **asparagus cookers** are available – tall narrow pans with an inner basket. The asparagus stems are placed, cut end down, in the basket and the pan is filled to a depth of 1–2 inches with water. This way the tough asparagus stems cook quickly in boiling water, while the delicate heads are done more slowly in the steam at the top of the pan. If no asparagus cooker is available, any tall pan such as the base of a double boiler can be used.

Use a steamer for best results when cooking vegetables; an adjustable rack ensures their easy removal.

Steam squash and other vegetables, or fish, poultry and puddings in a steamer

Steamed Stuffed Squash

$1\frac{1}{2}$ lb pattypan (scallop) squash

For filling
1 lb ground beef
2 tablespoons oil
1 onion, chopped
$\frac{3}{4}$ cup fresh white breadcrumbs
$\frac{1}{2}$ teaspoon thyme
1 tablespoon chopped parsley
salt and pepper

This recipe can also be used for large zucchini or yellow squash; halve them lengthwise, scoop out the seeds and proceed as below.

Method
Trim the stems from the squash and cut around the tops in a circle to remove a 'hat' about 2 inches in diameter. Scoop out the seeds with a teaspoon.

To make filling: heat oil and fry the onion until soft. Add beef and continue cooking, stirring constantly, until well browned. Stir in breadcrumbs with the herbs and plenty of salt and pepper. Fill this mixture into the squash and set the 'hats' on top.

Set squash in a steamer, cover and steam 25–35 minutes or until squash are tender.

Steamed Bass Duxelles

2 bass (about 2 lb each), cleaned, tails and fins trimmed
bunch of watercress (for garnish)
$\frac{1}{3}$ cup melted butter (for serving)
2 tablespoons chopped parsley (for serving)

For duxelles stuffing
2 cups ($\frac{1}{2}$ lb) mushrooms, finely chopped
1 shallot or scallion, finely chopped
2 tablespoons butter
2 tablespoons chopped parsley
salt and pepper

Method
Wash the fish and dry on paper towels.

To make duxelles stuffing: in a skillet cook shallot or scallion in butter until soft. Add mushrooms and cook over brisk heat for 2–3 minutes, stirring, until all moisture has evaporated. Stir in the parsley and add seasoning. Fill stuffing into the cavities of the fish.

Set fish on the rack of a fish kettle or on a wire rack in a roasting pan and add about $\frac{3}{4}$ inch water to the pan – the water should not touch the fish. Cover pan with the lid or with foil and simmer on top of the stove for 20–25 minutes or until the fish flakes easily. Add more water to the pan when necessary so it does not become dry.

Transfer fish to a platter and garnish it with watercress. Add parsley to the melted butter and serve this sauce separately, with boiled potatoes.

Calves' Liver Molds

$\frac{1}{2}$ lb calves' liver
1 shallot, or scallion, finely chopped
$\frac{1}{4}$ cup chopped fat bacon, or ham
1 large egg, beaten to mix
salt and pepper
2 tablespoons heavy cream
2 slices of lean cooked ham

For béchamel sauce
$\frac{3}{4}$ cup milk
$\frac{1}{2}$ bay leaf
pinch of ground mace
1 slice onion
4 peppercorns
1 tablespoon butter
1 tablespoon flour
salt and pepper

4 individual dariole molds, or 4 custard cups; 2 inch cookie cutter

Method
For sauce, infuse milk by bringing it almost to a boil with bay leaf, mace, onion and peppercorns; keep hot 5–7 minutes and strain. In a saucepan melt butter; when foaming, remove from heat and stir in flour. Pour in infused milk, return to heat and bring to a boil, stirring until thickened. Season, simmer 2 minutes and cool.

Have a steamer over a pan of boiling water ready.

Work liver twice through the fine blade of grinder with shallot and fat bacon or ham. Pound mixture with a mortar and pestle and stir in egg. Beat in cold béchamel sauce. Alternatively purée liver, onion, bacon, and egg with sauce in a blender. Season well and stir in the cream.

Thoroughly butter the molds or cups and place a round of cooked ham, stamped out with a cookie cutter, in the base of each one. Spoon liver mixture into the molds, cover each securely with a piece of brown paper and place in steamer. Cover and steam 15 minutes for molds, 20 minutes for custard cups, or until firm. Cool slightly. Slip a small knife inside around edge to loosen creams and turn onto a hot platter. Pour around a little sauce piquante and serve rest separately.

Sauce Piquante

1 shallot, or scallion, finely chopped
1 tablespoon butter
1 tablespoon flour
$\frac{3}{4}$ cup beef stock
1 teaspoon tomato paste
salt and pepper
2 teaspoons finely chopped gherkin pickles

To finish
squeeze of lemon juice
2 teaspoons finely chopped parsley
$\frac{1}{2}$ tablespoon butter

Method
Lightly brown shallot in butter, stir in flour and cook over medium heat; stirring, for 30 seconds or until golden. Take from heat and stir in stock with tomato paste. Bring the sauce to a boil and simmer 10 minutes or until glossy. If sauce is thicker than a gravy, add a little more stock. Add chopped pickles, remove from heat and add lemon juice, parsley, and lastly the butter; season to taste. Stir well and reheat without boiling.

HOW TO MAKE SPONGE PUDDINGS

Sponge puddings can be steamed or boiled. Whichever method is used, it is important to keep the water in the saucepan boiling constantly, and to refill it regularly.

To boil a pudding, a heatproof bowl containing the pudding mixture is covered with foil or a clean cloth and tied securely with string. Make sure there is enough water in the saucepan to cover the bowl completely.

To steam a pudding (in its bowl) without a steamer, the saucepan must be deep enough to allow room for the pudding to rise, and the boiling water in the pan should not come more than halfway up the sides of the bowl. As when boiling, the bowl should be filled with mixture and the foil or cloth covering must be firmly tied with string.

To avoid burning your hands, make a loop of string after tying so you can lift the bowl easily from the saucepan or steamer.

Dariole molds are about 3 inches high with a characteristic bucket shape. They are often used for cakes and puddings, particularly rum babas.

The quantities given in the following recipes are enough to serve 5–6 people

Valencia Pudding

1 cup seedless raisins
$\frac{3}{4}$ cup butter
grated rind and juice of $\frac{1}{2}$ lemon
$\frac{3}{4}$ cup sugar
3 eggs
$1\frac{1}{4}$ cups self-rising flour
pinch of salt

Charlotte mold, or heatproof bowl (1 quart capacity)

Method

Thoroughly butter the charlotte mold or bowl and have ready a steamer over a pan of boiling water.

Split and press enough raisins (skin side against the prepared mold or bowl) to cover the base and make a pattern on the sides. Cut remaining raisins in small pieces.

In a bowl, soften butter with lemon rind, add sugar and beat until mixture is light and fluffy. Beat in eggs, one at a time, with 1 teaspoon flour. Sift remaining flour with salt and fold into egg mixture with lemon juice and remaining raisins, using a metal spoon. Spoon carefully into the prepared mold or bowl. Cover with buttered foil (making a 1 inch pleat to allow the mixture to rise) and tie down with string. Steam for 2 hours or boil for $1\frac{1}{2}$ hours or until pudding is firm when pressed with a fingertip. Turn out onto a hot platter and spoon over a little sabayon sauce or serve with lemon hard sauce.

Sabayon Sauce

For 2 cup quantity
2 eggs
2 egg yolks
6 tablespoons sugar
$\frac{1}{4}$ cup sherry, or fruit juice

Method

Put all the ingredients in the top of a double boiler and whisk over hot but not boiling water, until sauce is thick and frothy. Do not overcook or it will separate. Serve warm.

Note: try not to make this sauce more than 15 minutes before serving. If it has to be prepared in advance, whisk it again for 1 minute before serving.

Lemon Hard Sauce

For $\frac{3}{4}$ cup quantity
6 tablespoons butter
grated rind of 1 lemon
$\frac{1}{4}$ cup confectioners' sugar
juice of $\frac{1}{2}$ lemon

Method

In a bowl, soften butter with lemon rind. Add confectioners' sugar, a little at a time, with lemon juice and beat until very light and fluffy. Pile in a small bowl and chill until very firm before serving.

Date Pudding

$\frac{3}{4}$ cup dates, pitted and chopped
1 cup self-rising flour
$\frac{1}{4}$ teaspoon cinnamon
$\frac{1}{4}$ teaspoon allspice
pinch of cloves
pinch of salt
6 tablespoons butter
$\frac{1}{2}$ cup fresh breadcrumbs
$\frac{1}{4}$ cup dark brown sugar
2 eggs
1 tablespoon honey
1–2 tablespoons milk

Charlotte mold, or heatproof bowl (1 quart capacity)

Method

Sift flour with spices and salt into a bowl. Cut in butter with a knife, then rub in with fingertips until mixture is crumbly. Stir in breadcrumbs, sugar and dates. Whisk eggs until mixed and stir in honey and milk, add to dry ingredients and mix thoroughly, adding extra milk if necessary to make a soft mixture that falls from the spoon.

Transfer mixture into the well-buttered mold or bowl, cover with buttered foil (making a 1 inch pleat in the center to allow the mixture to rise) and tie down with string. Steam $1\frac{1}{2}$–2 hours, or boil 1–$1\frac{1}{4}$ hours or until pudding is firm when pressed with a fingertip. Serve hot with sabayon sauce.

Chocolate Pudding

3 squares (3 oz) semi-sweet chocolate
¾ cup milk
1½ cups cake crumbs (the cake should not be too fresh)
¼ cup butter
¼ cup sugar
2 large eggs, separated
½ teaspoon vanilla
1 cup heavy cream, stiffly whipped (to serve)

8 dariole molds, or 8 custard cups

Method

Break chocolate into pieces and melt it in the milk over gentle heat. Bring to a boil and pour over cake crumbs in a bowl. Mix well with a fork and leave 20–30 minutes. Have ready a steamer over a pan of boiling water and butter molds or cups.

Soften butter in a bowl, add sugar and beat until light and fluffy. Beat in egg yolks and stir in soaked crumbs and vanilla. Beat egg whites until they form a stiff peak and fold them carefully into the chocolate mixture, using a metal spoon.

Divide mixture between buttered molds or cups, cover with foil, tie securely and steam 45 minutes, or boil 30 minutes, or until set (if done, the top will spring back when lightly pressed with a fingertip).

Turn out onto a hot platter, sprinkle with sugar and serve warm with whipped cream or hot chocolate sauce.

Chocolate Sauce

2 squares (2 oz) unsweetened chocolate
½ cup sugar
¾ cup water
1 teaspoon vanilla

Method

Dissolve sugar in water over gentle heat, bring to a boil and boil 5 minutes. Add chocolate, cut in pieces, and cook, stirring, until chocolate is melted. Take from heat and stir in vanilla.

Individual chocolate puddings with hot chocolate sauce

Danish raspberry shortcake, topped with rosettes of whipped cream, is ready to serve

A Simple Luncheon

For a celebration or just a simple lunch (it's all planned out for you in the TIMETABLE on page 70) try succulent baby lamb. Start the meal with salmon mousse, that calls for one of the best white wines; the town of Meursault in the southern half of Burgundy's 'Slope of Gold' produces a wide variety of classic whites known for their splendid bouquet and clean, dry taste. America's best white wine in the Burgundy tradition is Chardonnay – particularly when it comes from one of the top San Francisco Bay area vineyards. With the lamb, try a hearty but dry red wine from Pomerol, a district in the eastern half of France's famed Bordeaux region. A California wine – different but equally suitable – is the American original, Zinfandel.

Salmon Mousse
Cucumber Salad

Pot Roast Leg of Lamb
with Spring Vegetables

Danish Raspberry Shortcake

White wine – Meursault (Côte de Beaune)
or Chardonnay (California)

Red wine – Pomerol (Bordeaux)
or Zinfandel (California)

TIMETABLE

Day before
Make court bouillon; cook salmon and prepare béchamel sauce for mousse.
Make stock for lamb and refrigerate.
Make pastry and red currant glaze for shortcake.
Make aspic from consommé.
Complete salmon mousse, coating top with aspic when it is at the point of setting. Cover and refrigerate. If using frozen fruit for shortcake, leave to thaw overnight in refrigerator. Bake shortcake pastry and keep in airtight container.

Morning
If using canned vegetables, open and drain them or thaw and cook frozen vegetables.
Cover lamb with garlic and parsley butter and leave in casserole ready for cooking.

Assemble ingredients for final cooking from 10:15 a.m. for lunch around 1 p.m.

You will find that **cooking times** given in the individual recipes for these dishes have sometimes been adapted in the timetable to help you when cooking and serving this menu as a party meal.

Order of Work

10:15
Set oven at moderately hot (375°F). Place pastry on platter, arrange fruit, glaze it, decorate with cream and chill.

10:30
Start cooking lamb on top of stove. Make cucumber salad and refrigerate.

11:00
Add wine to lamb; when reduced, put casserole in oven. Check lamb after 30 minutes to see if the heat needs lowering.

11:45
Add fresh potatoes and carrots to casserole.

12:15
Add fresh beans and peas to casserole. Warm plates.

12:40
Strain gravy from lamb and add canned or frozen vegetables to casserole.
Turn oven to low and keep casserole hot.
Prepare sauce for lamb. Arrange meat and some vegetables on platter, and keep warm.

1:00
Serve salmon mousse.

Appetizer

Salmon Mousse

1 lb salmon steak
$\frac{1}{4}$ cup butter
$\frac{1}{4}$ cup heavy cream
2 tablespoons sherry
few drops of red food coloring (optional)

For court bouillon
2 cups water
juice of $\frac{1}{2}$ lemon, or $\frac{1}{2}$ cup white wine
$\frac{1}{2}$ teaspoon salt
6 peppercorns
bouquet garni

For béchamel sauce
$1\frac{1}{2}$ cups milk
1 bay leaf
$\frac{1}{4}$ teaspoon ground mace
6 peppercorns
1 slice of onion
3 tablespoons butter
3 tablespoons flour
salt

To finish
$\frac{1}{2}$ envelope gelatin
$\frac{3}{4}$ cup canned consommé
2 tablespoons sherry (optional)
$\frac{1}{2}$ cucumber, finely sliced
Melba toast (optional)

Soufflé dish ($1\frac{1}{2}$ quart capacity)

This mousse is very rich, so serve it in small portions with Melba toast and, if you like, a cucumber salad.

Method
For court bouillon, simmer all ingredients in a covered saucepan for 10 minutes and strain. Put salmon in a pan, pour over hot court bouillon and bring to a boil. Cover and simmer gently for 12–15 minutes or until salmon flakes easily. Cool, drain fish on paper towels and remove all skin and bones.

Watchpoint: the court bouillon must just 'tremble' throughout the cooking time. If you prefer to cook the salmon in the oven with the court bouillon, cover it with foil and bake at moderately low heat (325°F) for 20–25 minutes or until it flakes easily, basting often.

To prepare béchamel sauce: infuse milk by bringing it almost to a boil with bay leaf, mace, peppercorns and onion. Keep hot 5–7 minutes and then strain. In a saucepan melt the butter and, when foaming, remove from heat and stir in flour. Add infused milk and bring sauce to a boil, stirring constantly. Season to taste and simmer 2 minutes. Remove from heat and cool.

Cream $\frac{1}{4}$ cup butter and whip cream until it holds a shape. Pound salmon in a bowl with a wooden spoon or end of a rolling pin, or in a mortar and pestle.

Watchpoint: pounding the salmon breaks down the fibers of the fish so it will hold the sauce and butter without separating.

Beat cold béchamel sauce and butter into salmon and taste for seasoning. Fold in cream and sherry, taste for seasoning and add a few drops of red coloring if mixture is very pale. Turn mousse into the soufflé dish, smooth the top with a palette knife and chill 30 minutes or until firm.

To make aspic, sprinkle gelatin over 3 tablespoons consommé in a small saucepan; stand 5 minutes or until spongy. Then dissolve over a pan of hot water and stir into remaining consommé. If you like, a little sherry or brandy can be added to the aspic to improve the flavor.

Spoon a thin layer of aspic over salmon and chill; when

set, arrange cucumber slices on top, dipping each slice first in liquid aspic. When this garnish is set in position, fill dish to top with remaining aspic. (Instructions for making true aspic will be given in a future Volume.)

When the mousse is firm, pour on a thin layer of liquid aspic; when set, dip cucumber slices in more aspic and arrange on top

Cucumber Salad

2 cucumbers
salt
black pepper, freshly ground
sugar (to taste)
1 tablespoon white wine or cider vinegar

Method

Peel cucumber, if preferred, slice thinly and sprinkle with salt; leave the slices pressed between 2 plates to draw out the juices (dégorger) in a cool place for 1 hour. Tip away any liquid and rinse off excess salt. Add pepper, sugar and vinegar and pile salad in a serving bowl.

Entrée

Pot Roast Leg of Lamb
with Spring Vegetables

4-5 lb leg of lamb

$\frac{1}{4}$ cup butter
$\frac{1}{2}$ clove garlic, crushed (optional)
1 tablespoon chopped parsley
$\frac{1}{2}$ cup white wine
salt
black pepper, freshly ground
10 small new potatoes, peeled, or 1 can potatoes
bunch of baby carrots, or 1 can whole carrots
1 cup shelled fresh peas, or 1 package frozen peas, cooked
1 cup shelled baby lima beans, or 1 package frozen lima beans, cooked
1 teaspoon sugar
1 tablespoon flour
6 tablespoons light cream

For stock
shank bone of lamb
1 onion
1 stick celery
1 carrot
6 peppercorns
salt

Method

For stock, place shank bone of lamb in a saucepan with remaining stock ingredients and add water to cover. Put lid on pan and simmer 2 hours or until stock is very concentrated. Strain.

Trim any skin and fat from leg of lamb. Cream the butter in a bowl with a wooden spoon and work in garlic and parsley; spread over the lamb and leave 15 minutes. Then place in a large flameproof casserole, cover, and cook over gentle heat for 30 minutes. Shake the casserole occasionally to prevent lamb from sticking. At the end of this time the meat should have changed color from pink to grey but should not be brown. Set oven at moderately hot (375°F).

Add wine to casserole and simmer gently, uncovered, until reduced by one-third. Add $\frac{1}{2}$ cup of stock from shank bone and season. Cover and roast in preheated oven for 1–1$\frac{1}{2}$ hours or until meat is very tender.

Watchpoint: check meat after 30 minutes' cooking. If the casserole is of cast iron, as opposed to flameproof earthenware, you will probably need to lower oven heat to 325°F because the meat should cook gently.

If vegetables are fresh, add potatoes and carrots to the pan at this point, 1 hour before end of cooking time, and peas and beans 30 minutes before end of cooking. Strain and reserve gravy from casserole, leaving meat and vegetables; if canned or frozen ones are used, add vegetables at this point. Turn oven to low, add sugar to casserole, cover and keep hot in oven.

For sauce, skim fat from cooking liquid, mix with flour and stir back into liquid. Heat in a small pan, stirring, until boiling; simmer 2–3 minutes. Add cream and reheat. Taste for seasoning.

Arrange meat on a platter, surrounded by vegetables (add enough of them to look attractive without being in the way of the carver) and spoon over a little sauce. Spoon rest of sauce over remaining vegetables; serve separately.

Pot roast leg of lamb, with tender spring vegetables, is an ideal dish for entertaining

Dessert

Danish Raspberry Shortcake

1 pint fresh raspberries, or 2 packages frozen raspberries
$\frac{1}{2}$ cup red currant glaze (see page 55)
$\frac{1}{2}$ cup heavy cream, stiffly whipped

For pastry
1 cup flour
6 tablespoons butter
6 tablespoons confectioners' sugar
1 egg yolk
$\frac{1}{2}$ teaspoon vanilla

If using frozen raspberries, thaw, separate carefully, and drain on paper towels. However, even with careful treatment frozen raspberries tend to be soft and strawberries frozen without sugar, are an excellent substitute. Unpack the strawberries while still frozen and place them on a baking sheet not touching each other, to thaw in the refrigerator. When thawed they will be quite firm. Otherwise use any firm fruit, like peaches or pineapple, with an apricot jam glaze (see page 55).

Method
First prepare pastry: sift flour onto a board or marble slab, make a well in the center and add the other pastry ingredients. Work to a smooth dough with the fingertips of one hand, drawing in flour gradually; chill pastry for 30 minutes. Set oven at moderately hot (375°F).

On a baking sheet, roll or pat out pastry to a circle $\frac{1}{4}$ inch thick and 7–8 inches in diameter. Trim edges neatly, using a pan lid or plate as a guide, and bake in preheated oven for 12–15 minutes or until pastry is set and deep cream-colored, but not brown.

Cool pastry and brush with glaze. Arrange raspberries on top and brush with remaining glaze. Chill and, just before serving, decorate the edge with whipped cream, preferably piped in rosettes through a pastry bag fitted with a star tube.

To Pipe Whipped Cream

Use a pastry bag made of canvas or nylon with a waterproof finish. This is fitted with a $\frac{1}{2}$ inch star tube.

Whip cream until it is stiff but still falls from a spoon – if it is too stiff, it will curdle as it is forced through the tube.

To pipe a rosette: hold the pastry bag upright in one hand, and using the other hand to guide the nozzle, move the tube in a clockwise circle, pressing the pastry bag firmly and continuously.

Make one or more circles of whipped cream, depending on the height of rosette required

HOW TO MAKE OMELETS

An omelet is a boon to busy cooks; it is quick and simple to make, calls for few ingredients and is delicious whether plain or filled with any of a wide variety of fillings. The secret of a successful omelet lies in using really fresh eggs and a good omelet pan, which should be kept for omelets only; if used for frying other foods, it must be washed and this can cause omelets to stick.

A true omelet pan is made either of thick aluminum or cast iron, with or without a non-stick finish. The characteristic curved sides of the pan make an omelet easier to turn out and give it a better shape.

Pans come in different sizes, but a 7–8 inch diameter pan is generally useful as it will take a 4 egg omelet, which serves two people. A large, heavy pan is more awkward to handle and the omelet itself is not easy to manipulate.

When buying an omelet pan which doesn't have a non-stick finish, treat it before use as follows: wash well, dry and cover bottom with salt and oil. Stand for 12 hours, then heat oil until very hot. Take from heat, pour away oil and wipe pan thoroughly with paper towels while still hot; the inside should never be washed after use, but wiped with a damp cloth dipped in salt. This will season the pan and prevent an omelet from sticking.

Omelets

For a plain omelet: pour eggs into the foaming butter

Stir eggs with flat of the fork

Start to turn the omelet over

Fold it over, with pan tilted

Tip the omelet onto a plate

OMELETS

There are two types of omelet, the plain, or French omelet, and the fluffy, or soufflé one (the latter kind will be described in a future lesson on soufflés). French omelets are generally savory, either plain or filled; here they are usually served as a light lunch or supper dish, although in France they are a popular appetizer as well. You can transform a plain omelet into a dessert by filling it with fruit conserve or jam (preferably homemade) although sweet flavorings are more suited to a soufflé omelet.

Plain Omelet

4 eggs
1½ tablespoons cold water
salt
black pepper, freshly ground
2 tablespoons butter

7–8 inch omelet pan

Method
Break eggs into a bowl and beat well with a fork. When yolks and whites are broken up, add water and seasoning (this should be done just before cooking). Heat pan on medium heat, add butter in two pieces and, as soon as it is foaming, pour in egg mixture. Leave 10–15 seconds before stirring around slowly with the flat of a fork. Stir once or twice around pan, then cook for another 5–6 seconds.

Lift up the edge of omelet to let any remaining raw egg run onto the hot pan. (Some people like omelets to be soft in the center, others prefer them cooked through so the length of cooking time depends on your preference.) Tilt the pan away from you and fold the omelet over to the far side. Change your grip on the pan so that the handle runs up the palm of your hand. Take a warmed dish or plate in your other hand, tilt it slightly and tip the omelet onto it, folding under the other edge, with a metal spatula. Serve at once.

Herb Omelet
(Fines Herbes Omelet)

This is a delicious omelet, especially in summer when herbs are fresh.

Method
Make a plain 4-egg omelet, but before pouring mixture into the pan, add 2 tablespoons chopped herbs (tarragon, chervil and chives are the classic combination, but parsley, thyme and marjoram also can be used). Snip chives finely with scissors (chopping bruises them). The mixture should be quite green with herbs.

Stuffed Omelets

Make in the same way as a plain omelet and spread the filling mixture quickly across the omelet before folding. A little of the filling, such as tomato or mushroom, can be reserved to spoon over the center of the omelet when turned out.

Almost any cooked fish, chicken or vegetable mixture is good in a stuffed omelet – here are some suggestions using a 4-egg quantity (serving 2 people).

Cheese Omelet

Method
Make a plain 4-egg omelet and, just before folding it, scatter 2–3 tablespoons of grated or finely diced cheese thickly over it. A mature Cheddar or Gruyère cheese has the best flavor.

Potato Omelet

1–2 medium potatoes, diced small
½ tablespoon butter
few leaves of rosemary (optional)
salt and pepper

Method
This omelet can be made with cooked or raw potatoes. Brown potatoes in butter, cooking them long enough if raw to be sure they are soft before removing from heat. Add rosemary while frying, but salt and pepper at end of cooking. Make a plain omelet and spoon in potatoes before folding.

Tomato Omelet

2 medium tomatoes, peeled seeded and coarsely chopped
½ tablespoon butter
salt and pepper
2 teaspoons chopped mint (for garnish)

Method
Sauté tomatoes in butter in a pan for 1–2 minutes. Season well. Add a good sprinkling of mint before spooning into a plain omelet. Don't overcook tomatoes.

Ripe fresh tomatoes are also good when added uncooked to an omelet. Simply peel, seed and chop them and sprinkle with seasoning.

Chicken Liver Omelet

2–3 chicken livers
½ tablespoon butter
2 teaspoons flour
1 tablespoon sherry
3–4 tablespoons stock
½ teaspoon tomato paste (optional)
salt and pepper

Method
Sauté chicken livers in butter until brown but still pink inside. Slice, sprinkle with flour and return to pan. Add sherry, moisten with a little stock, bring to a boil and simmer 2–3 minutes. Add tomato paste and taste for seasoning. Make a plain omelet and spoon in mixture before folding.

Mushroom Omelet

1 cup (¼ lb) mushrooms, sliced or quartered
½ tablespoon butter
½ tablespoon flour
3–4 tablespoons stock, or water
salt and pepper
squeeze of lemon juice

Method
Sauté mushrooms in butter in a pan for 2–3 minutes or until tender. Stir in flour, add liquid and seasoning and stir until boiling. Then add lemon juice. Consistency of the mushroom filling should be creamy. Make a plain omelet; spoon in mushroom mixture before folding.

The quantities in the omelet recipes given on pages 76 and 79 are for serving 2 people.

Omelets

Tomato omelet is a delicious and simple dish to make. Serve garnished with chopped mint

Omelet Grimaldi is stuffed with tomato fondue and spinach purée just before folding

Bacon and Potato Omelet (Omelet Bonne Femme)

2–3 slices of bacon, diced
2 medium potatoes, diced small
1 small onion, finely sliced
½ tablespoon butter
salt and pepper

Method
Melt butter in a pan and add bacon, potatoes and onion. Season, cover pan and cook slowly for 7–8 minutes, or until potatoes and onion are tender and lightly browned. Stir occasionally. Make a plain omelet and spoon in the mixture before folding.

Bacon and Croûton Omelet

3–4 slices of bacon, diced
2 slices of bread, diced, with crusts removed
½ tablespoon butter

Method
To make croûtons, fry diced bread in butter in a pan until golden. Remove and fry bacon until crisp. Drain and combine with croûtons. Make a plain omelet; spoon in bacon mixture before folding.

Bonne femme literally means good woman; it is often used to describe homey, traditional food and can be applied to dishes as varied as beef broth garnished with vegetables, or a rich white sauce flavored with mushrooms. A bonne femme garnish usually refers to onion and bacon, with or without potato.

Truffle Omelet

Make a plain 4-egg omelet, but before pouring the mixture into the pan, add 1 small can of truffle pieces, chopped, with the liquid.

Truffles are one of the most luxurious foods in the world, and the combination of truffles and eggs, in an omelet or scrambled, is superb.

Truffles are coal-black fungi that grow underground attached to the roots of stunted oak trees, and no one has ever succeeded in cultivating them. The aroma and flavor of truffles is intense, so very few are needed to season a dish. They are sold here in small cans, whole or in pieces.

Zucchini Omelet

2 zucchini, thinly sliced
1 tablespoon olive oil
1 scallion, finely chopped
½ clove garlic, crushed
1 medium tomato, peeled, seeded, and chopped
pinch of thyme
1 teaspoon chopped parsley
salt and pepper

Method
In a skillet heat oil and sauté scallion with garlic until soft. Add zucchini with tomato, herbs, and salt and pepper to taste. Cover pan and cook gently for 8 minutes or until zucchini is tender. Make a plain omelet and spoon in the zucchini mixture before folding.

Omelet Grimaldi

Plain 4-egg omelet

For tomato fondue
2 ripe tomatoes, peeled, seeded and chopped, or 1½ cups (¾ lb) canned Italian-type tomatoes, drained and crushed
2 tablespoons olive oil
2 shallots or scallions, finely chopped
bouquet garni
salt and pepper

For spinach purée
¾ lb fresh spinach or 1 package frozen spinach
1–2 tablespoons cream

Method
To make tomato fondue: in a skillet, heat oil and fry shallot or scallion until soft. Add tomatoes, bouquet garni and seasoning and cook, stirring, until the mixture is rich and thick. Discard bouquet garni.

To make spinach purée: wash spinach thoroughly and cook in boiling salted water for 5 minutes or until just tender. Cook frozen spinach according to package directions. Drain and press well with a spoon or plate to remove as much water as possible. Work through a sieve and add cream or purée in a blender with cream.

Make a plain omelet and spoon in hot tomato and spinach mixtures before folding. Or fill omelet with spinach mixture and spoon tomato mixture down center of omelet after folding.

Oyster Omelet

½ pint standard oysters, shucked
2 tablespoons butter
2 tablespoons brandy
2 egg yolks
¼ cup heavy cream
pinch of cayenne
salt and pepper

Method
Drain oysters and coarsely chop them. Melt butter in a pan and sauté the oysters quickly for 1 minute. Add brandy and cook 1 minute more. In a bowl combine egg yolks and cream and stir into oyster mixture, off the heat. Stir over low heat until the mixture thickens, but do not boil. Season to taste with cayenne, salt and pepper. Make a plain omelet and spoon in the oyster mixture before folding.

Crab Meat Omelet

¾ cup (⅓ lb) flaked, cooked crab meat
1 tablespoon butter
1 shallot, or scallion, finely chopped
1 teaspoon flour
½ teaspoon chopped tarragon
1 teaspoon chopped parsley
2 tablespoons sherry
¼ cup heavy cream
salt and pepper

Method
In a pan heat butter and sauté shallot until soft. Stir in crab meat with flour, herbs and sherry and cook gently for 5 minutes or until crab meat is very hot. Stir in cream and season to taste. Make a plain omelet and spoon in the crab meat mixture before folding.

HOW TO BONE, CUT UP & CARVE POULTRY

Chicken, duck, goose, turkey and rock Cornish game hen are all classed as poultry and they fall into two natural categories: either they have dark, rich flesh or they are white-fleshed with little natural fat. Duck, like goose, has a dark flesh, thickly covered with fat under the skin. Both are best roasted, or pot roasted to keep the skin crisp, and accompanied by a sharp sauce, such as the traditional orange, or a fresh-tasting salad, to offset their richness and give contrasting flavor.

Chicken, turkey and rock Cornish game hen are in the second category and can be cooked in many different ways; the most popular are to broil, roast, fry or cook them in a casserole.

When choosing a fresh bird, look for a plump breast, a good creamy color and a small body with enough fat under the skin to give flavor. The bird is weighed after plucking and drawing (removing the innards). Cleaned giblets (neck, gizzard, heart and liver) should be included inside the bird.

A frozen bird has the unfrozen weight clearly marked. Thaw it slowly in the refrigerator for 24 hours. Never unfreeze it in hot water as this toughens the flesh. To thaw a bird quickly, put it into a large bowl under slowly running cold water. On the following pages are step-by-step photographs of boning and cutting up chickens, together with diagrams showing you how to carve a duck or a goose, and instructions for splitting and boning baby chickens and rock Cornish game hens.

Types of Chicken

Chickens vary considerably in size and flavor according to their age.

Broilers are the babies of the family, aged from 7–12 weeks. They vary in weight from 1–2½ lb although the smallest, which serve only one person, are very hard to find. The average broiler serves two. They are best broiled, pot roasted or roasted.

Fryers weigh up to 3½ lb and, being more mature than broilers, have a stronger flavor. They may be roasted or pot roasted and are ideal for a sauté as the pieces are not too large. One bird is enough for 2–3 people, depending on the method of cooking.

Roasters are aged between 5–10 months and they weigh anywhere from 3–6 lb. They are the most popular size of chicken for a family, serving 3–6 people, and you can boil, pot roast or roast them, serving them with an appropriate sauce and garnish.

Capons are unsexed male birds specially fattened for the table. They are large, weighing up to 9 lb, and have plenty of plump white breast meat. Roast or poach them for about 2 hours for use as a cold buffet dish.

Fowls are mature hens – meaty, full of flavor, though tending to fat. These are the traditional birds for boiling and they make excellent soups, casseroles, cold dishes and mousses.

French roasting is a good method of cooking chicken, duck or turkey, particularly if the bird is to be served cold, because the flesh remains succulent and full of flavor. The bird is roasted in butter and basted with a little strong stock (in contrast to regular roasting, when no liquid is used and the flesh tends to be dry).

If **ready-trussed poultry** is not available, or if a recipe requires a bird to be trussed after it has been boned and stuffed, check the step-by-step diagrams of trussing and also of carving on pages 20–21.

Boning a chicken

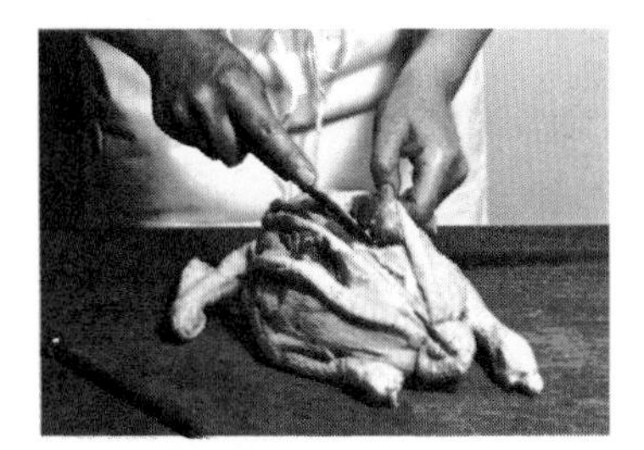

1 Remove the trussing string or skewer. With a sharp knife, slit the skin along the backbone. Work skin and flesh from this area of carcass with the small knife until leg joint is reached; sever it

2 Hold the end of the ball joint firmly in one hand. Cut away flesh with knife and scrape the thigh bone completely clean, always working from the inside of the leg

3 Continue cleaning the drumstick until the whole leg bone is free of flesh. Now cut the leg bone from the flesh and repeat this cleaning process with the other leg, freeing the leg bone of all flesh

4 Sever the wing joint from carcass, leaving bone attached to chicken meat. Still using knife, separate white meat from breastbone, leaving carcass intact; stop there. Now free the other wing and breast

5 Carefully cut away skin from top of breastbone without splitting skin; keep both sides of bird attached so that it remains in one piece for stuffing

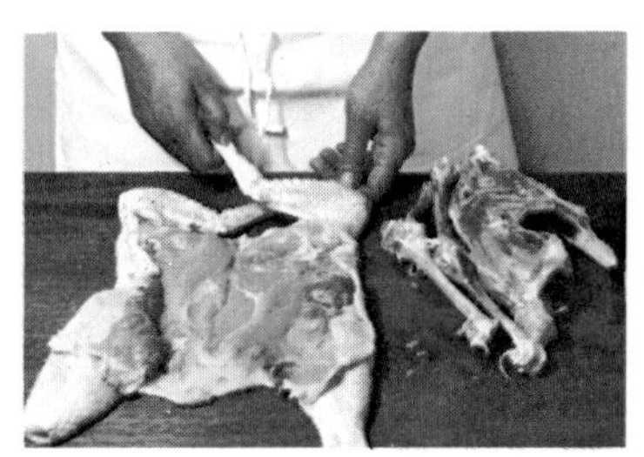

6 Lay the chicken flat ready for the stuffing to spread over the cut surfaces. Then sew up or secure with poultry pins and string; it is now ready to truss

Boning a small bird

A small bird can be completely boned and stuffed, but the shape is better if it is only partly boned, leaving the leg bone in a small broiling chicken and both legs and breastbone in a rock Cornish game hen.

1 Remove any trussing strings or skewers, turn bird onto breastbone; with a small, sharp knife, slit skin along backbone.
2 With tail of bird towards you, ease flesh and skin away from carcass on left-hand side. Work evenly with short, sharp strokes, keeping the edge of the knife against ribs. Sever leg and wing through ball and socket joints.
3 Turn bird around, and repeat on other side.
4 Cut away rib and backbone with scissors.
5 Spread stuffing over cut surfaces of bird. Sew up underside, or secure with poultry pins and string; truss.

Cutting up a raw chicken

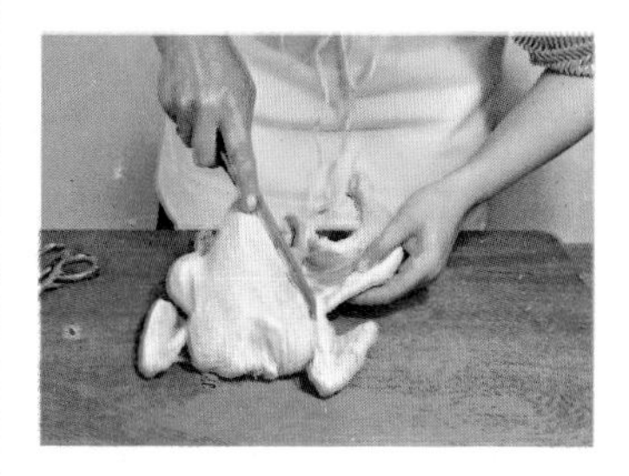

1 Hold chicken firmly on board with one hand. With a sharp knife, sever skin between leg and breast. Then, pressing flat of knife against carcass, take leg in other hand and bend it sharply outwards until bone breaks away from carcass

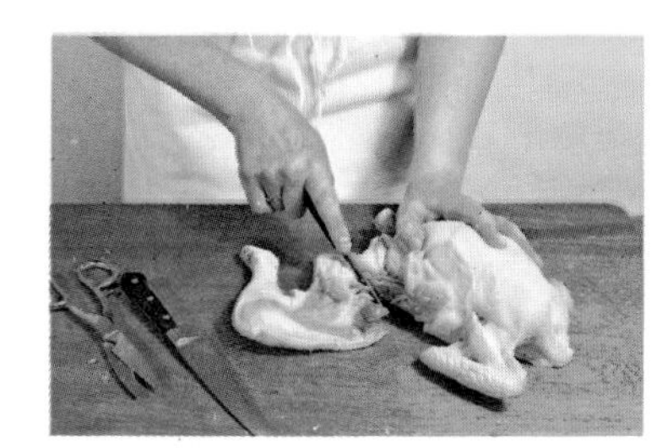

2 Slide knife around leg joint, cutting down towards the tail, keeping it between oyster and backbone. The leg is now separated from carcass and has oyster bone (from beneath carcass) attached. Remove remaining leg in the same way

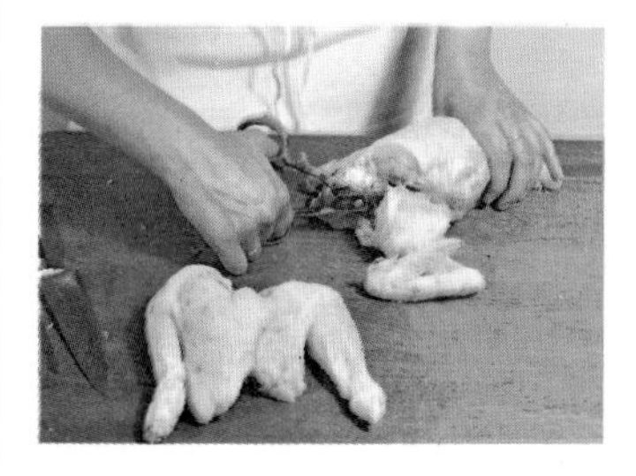

3 Make slantwise cut with knife halfway up breast across to top of wishbone from neck to end of wing joint. With scissors or poultry shears, cut down through wishbone and ribs to detach wing with a good portion of breast

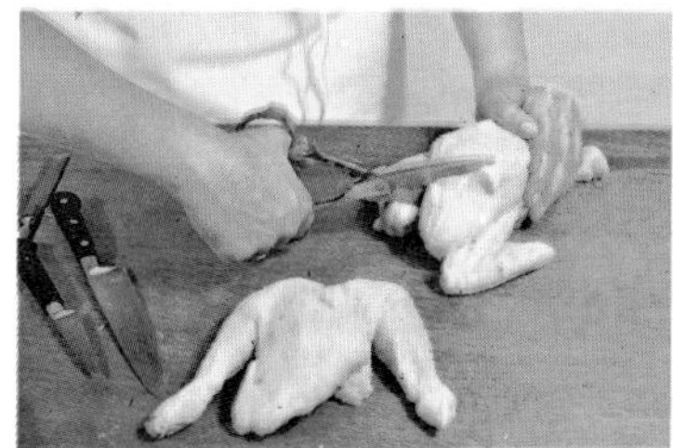

4 Twist wing pinion out and tuck it under this breast meat to hold the piece flat. This makes for even browning of meat. To obtain both wings of even size, make slantwise cuts at the same time, then detach other wing in the same way

5 Cut away the breast meat in one piece with the scissors. All that is now left of the carcass are the ribs, the backbone and the tail.

6 The chicken pieces are ready for cooking. The carcass may be cut in half and then sautéed with the other pieces to give the finished dish more flavor

Sautéed or broiled chicken
If you sauté, broil, or make a similar dish using pieces of chicken, the pieces will look more attractive if you cut up the bird yourself. Ready-cut pieces include backbone and won't look so neat. When cutting up a bird, part of the carcass bone must be included with the wing and breast pieces, otherwise the flesh shrinks during cooking.

In some recipes a chicken is browned whole, then divided as above; however, the legs are always divided after cooking, as for a roast chicken.

For a sauté, legs are left whole and knuckle bone is trimmed after cooking.

Spatchcock Cornish Game Hens

4 rock Cornish game hens
black pepper, freshly ground
lemon juice
6 tablespoons butter, melted

For garnish
watercress
lemon quarters
straw potatoes (see right)

4 small skewers (6–8 inches long)

Spatchcock denotes any small bird which is split down the back before broiling. **Spitchcock** refers to the same process with eel.

Method

With scissors, cut through backs of birds. Cut away the backbone, lay the hens flat on a chopping block skin side upwards and press down sharply with the palm of the hand so the breastbone cracks and the bird lies flat. Run a skewer through the legs to keep the birds flat. Sprinkle them with a little pepper and lemon juice and brush with some of the melted butter, keeping some for basting. Leave 30 minutes before broiling.

Heat broiler. Place hens on broiler rack, skin side up, and cook slowly until well browned, brushing with butter from time to time. When brown, turn over and continue to broil on other side, allowing about 7 minutes on each side.

Arrange cooked hens on a platter, pour over any juices from the broiler pan and garnish with watercress, lemon quarters and straw potatoes.

Chicken en Cocotte Grand'mere

2 small broilers, 2–2½ lb each (½ chicken per person)
3–4 tablespoons butter
¼ cup sherry
bouquet garni
1–1¼ cups chicken stock
2 teaspoons arrowroot mixed to a paste with 2 tablespoons water
salt and pepper
2 teaspoons mixed chopped herbs (parsley, thyme, and tarragon or basil)

For stuffing
2–3 shallots, or scallions, finely chopped
¼ cup butter
1 cup (½ lb) cooked ham, ground
1 cup fresh white breadcrumbs
1 teaspoon thyme
1 teaspoon chopped parsley
salt and pepper
1 egg, beaten to mix

For garnish
¼ lb piece of bacon, diced
12 small onions, peeled
1 lb small new potatoes, peeled

Method

Bone each chicken, removing ribs but leaving leg and wing bones.

For stuffing: cook shallots in butter until soft. Add to ham with breadcrumbs and herbs. Season well and stir in egg to bind. Spread mixture over chickens, sew up or secure with poultry pins and string, then truss into shape. Melt butter for chickens in a deep pan and brown birds slowly on all sides. Pour off any excess fat, reserving it for the garnish. Add sherry and bouquet garni to chickens, cover pan and cook over moderate heat on top of the stove or bake in a moderate oven (350°F) for 30 minutes or until tender.

For garnish: blanch bacon with onions and potatoes in boiling water for 5 minutes; drain well. Then brown in butter reserved from cooking chickens and add to pan with chickens for last 5 minutes of cooking.

Take out chickens, cut in half and arrange on a platter; remove garnish with a slotted spoon and reserve. Add stock to juices in pan and boil 2–3 minutes to dissolve them Thicken sauce by stirring the arrowroot paste, or kneaded butter, into hot sauce and cooking until just thick. Season, add chopped herbs and the garnish. Spoon this mixture over chickens and serve.

A liaison can be a mixture of butter and flour (roux), cornstarch or arrowroot, which is used to thicken a sauce or soup. The egg yolk and cream liaison which is used in velouté sauce not only thickens but also enriches the mixture.

Straw Potatoes

Peel 1 lb potatoes, square off the sides, as for French fries. Cut into slices ⅛ inch thick, then into matchsticks, ⅛ inch wide. Soak in cold water for 30 minutes and dry thoroughly on paper towels or a cloth. Heat a pan of deep fat to hot (350°F). Place the potatoes in a frying basket and fry 3–4 minutes or until soft. Lift out, heat fat to very hot (375°F) and cook potatoes for about 1 minute longer or until 'straws' are golden-brown and crisp. Drain well, sprinkle with salt and serve at once.

These straw potatoes are particularly good with spatchcock Cornish game hens and other game dishes.

Fresh Breadcrumbs

The easiest way to make fresh breadcrumbs is in the blender. Cut sliced white bread into cubes, removing the crust. Reduce these to crumbs, 1–2 slices at a time, in the blender at a moderately high speed.

If you have no blender, rub stale pieces of bread through a flat, wire sieve.

Chicken Parisienne

3–3$\frac{1}{2}$ lb roasting chicken
salt and pepper
$\frac{1}{4}$ cup butter
$\frac{3}{4}$ cup stock
$\frac{1}{4}$ cup sherry

For stuffing
2 tablespoons butter
1 shallot, or scallion, finely chopped
1 cup ($\frac{1}{2}$ lb) cooked ham, finely chopped
$\frac{1}{2}$ lb ground veal
$\frac{1}{4}$ cup fresh breadcrumbs
1 tablespoon chopped mixed herbs (parsley, thyme, rosemary and basil)
1 egg, beaten to mix

For velouté sauce and liaison
2 tablespoons butter
2 tablespoons flour
1$\frac{1}{4}$ cups chicken stock
1 egg yolk
1 cup light cream
1 cup ($\frac{1}{4}$ lb) mushrooms, thinly sliced
1 tablespoon butter
squeeze of lemon juice

Method

First prepare stuffing: melt butter in a small pan and cook shallot or scallion until soft; cool. Combine ham with veal, breadcrumbs and herbs. Add shallot, season well and stir in the beaten egg to bind the mixture.

Bone chicken, rub the inside with salt and pepper and spread with the stuffing. Sew up with string or secure with poultry pins and truss firmly (see page 20).

Set in a roasting pan, rub bird well with butter and pour stock and sherry around. Roast in a hot oven (400°F) for 1$\frac{1}{2}$ hours or until a skewer inserted in the center is hot to the touch when withdrawn after 1 minute. Baste and turn bird every 20 minutes during cooking.

Meanwhile prepare the sauce: in a saucepan melt butter, stir in flour and cook over medium heat, stirring, until lightly colored. Take pan from heat, add stock and bring to a boil, stirring continuously. Simmer 3–4 minutes and set aside. To cook the mushrooms, melt 1 tablespoon butter in a pan and sauté the mushrooms over gentle heat until tender, adding a squeeze of lemon juice to keep them white; reserve.

Make a liaison by beating the egg yolk lightly and stirring the cream into it. Just before serving, reheat sauce, blend a little into the liaison and stir this mixture back into the remaining sauce. Reheat carefully without boiling, stirring until sauce thickens slightly. Add mushrooms and taste for seasoning.

When chicken is cooked, remove the pins and trussing string and carve in slices. Arrange on a platter, spoon over a little of the sauce and serve the rest separately.

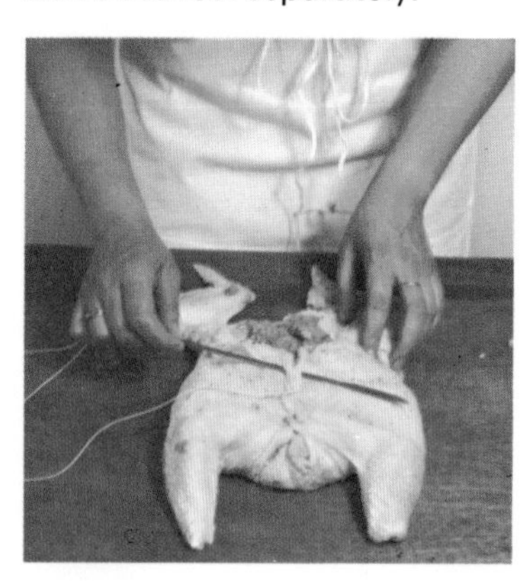

Above: for chicken Parisienne, first bone the bird; when this is done, lay it flat, rub the insides with salt and pepper and fill with stuffing. Draw the flaps of skin together over the stuffing and secure with poultry pins or sew with string

Above: after sewing, reshape and truss the bird. Remember to press the legs well down into the sides of the bird in order to plump out the breast, so the cooked bird looks more attractive

Chicken Dijonnaise

2 broiling chickens, 2–2$\frac{1}{2}$ lb each
$\frac{1}{4}$ cup butter
$\frac{3}{4}$ cup chicken stock
salt
pepper, freshly ground
2 teaspoons flour
grated rind and juice of $\frac{1}{2}$ orange
2 teaspoons Dijon-style mustard
1 tablespoon heavy cream (optional)
bunch of watercress (for garnish)

Method

In a large flameproof casserole, heat half the butter until foaming. Add chickens with $\frac{1}{4}$ cup stock and season. Cover and cook on a low to medium heat or in a moderate oven (350°F) for 30 minutes or until birds are tender, turning them occasionally.

Remove chickens and reserve the pan juices. Split chickens and trim away the backbones; arrange them for broiling on a heatproof platter.

For sauce: stir flour into butter and juices left in casserole, add remaining stock and heat until boiling, stirring continuously. Simmer 2 minutes, strain and keep warm.

Sprinkle chickens with orange juice, scatter with a little more salt and pepper. Melt remaining butter and spoon it over birds; broil them under a preheated broiler for 5 minutes or until crisp and golden. Add mustard and grated orange rind to sauce, with cream if used, and taste for seasoning. Pour sauce around chickens and garnish with watercress.

Splitting a Raw Broiler

1 Hold bird firmly on board with one hand; make a cut with a sharp knife through skin and flesh on top of breast.
2 Split in half with scissors, starting at wishbone, cutting through on one side of backbone. When divided, trim away backbone from other half of bird.
3 Trim the knuckle end of each drumstick and ends of wing pinions after cooking.

To Split a Cooked Broiler

Lift bird carefully from pan onto a board. Cut and draw out trussing strings before splitting as above.

For chicken Dijonnaise, make a sauce with the grated rind and juice of an orange and Dijon-style mustard and garnish with watercress.

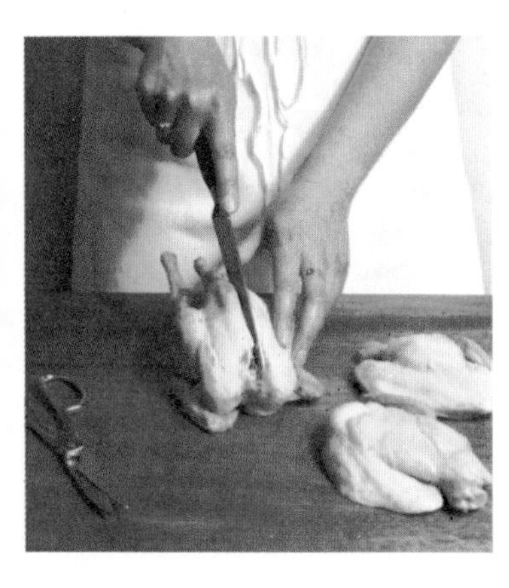

Before broiling the birds for chicken Dijonnaise, first split each one down the breastbone using a very sharp knife. Hold each bird firmly while cutting through bone with shears

Trim away the backbone from the chicken halves with poultry shears

Dijon-style mustard is made from white and black powdered mustard seeds. These are mixed with verjuice (the acid juice from large unripened grapes) in place of vinegar, sometimes with the addition of a few herbs.

Chicken Vichy

$3\frac{1}{2}$–4 lb roasting chicken
5–6 carrots
3 tablespoons butter
juice of $\frac{1}{2}$ small lemon
$\frac{1}{4}$ cup chicken stock
salt and pepper
1 teaspoon chopped parsley

For béchamel sauce
$1\frac{1}{2}$ cups milk
1 bay leaf
pinch of ground mace
1 slice of onion
6 peppercorns
2 tablespoons butter
2 tablespoons flour
salt and pepper

Method

Truss chicken and slice carrots in thin rounds.

Melt butter in a large flameproof casserole on top of stove, add chicken, brown it well on all sides and remove.

Reduce heat under casserole, add carrots, cover and cook slowly. Cut the chicken into 5 pieces.

When carrots have absorbed the butter in the casserole, pour over lemon juice and stock, add chicken pieces and season lightly. Cover with a tight fitting lid and cook over a low to medium heat or in a moderate oven (350°F) for 40 minutes or until tender.

Prepare béchamel sauce: infuse the milk by bringing it almost to a boil with bay leaf, mace, onion and peppercorns and keeping hot 5–7 minutes. Strain. In a saucepan melt butter and, when foaming, stir in flour off heat. Add infused milk and bring the sauce to a boil, stirring. Season to taste and simmer 2 minutes.

Take chicken from the casserole with a slotted spoon. Trim the pieces, and put them on a platter with the carrots and keep hot. Pour juices from the casserole into the sauce, bring to a boil and taste for seasoning. Add parsley and spoon over the chicken.

Preparing Duck and Goose

In most large cities, ducks and ducklings are available all year, although you will find fresh geese only at Thanksgiving and in winter. A duck or goose, being shallow breasted, will not serve as many people as a chicken or turkey of similar weight. A 5 lb duck serves four people.

Roast both duck and goose in a moderately hot oven (375°F) or on a spit. Spread a little butter on the breast (not necessary if bird is plump) and cook on a rack in a roasting pan and prick the skin so the fat can drain; baste bird every 20 minutes to brown and crisp skin. Pour excess fat from pan when necessary.

Roasting times: 15 minutes per lb plus 15 minutes more. The bird is done when no pink juice runs out when the thigh is pierced with a fork or when a meat thermometer inserted in the thickest part of the thigh registers 185°F.

Braised Duck with Olives

5 lb duck
2 tablespoons butter
1 medium onion, sliced
$\frac{1}{4}$ cup port
1 teaspoon paprika
$1\frac{1}{4}$ cups chicken stock
bouquet garni
salt and pepper
2 tomatoes peeled, quartered and cut in strips
2 teaspoons flour
12 large green olives, pitted, or stuffed with pimiento and drained
parsley (for garnish)

Method

Brown duck in butter for 10–15 minutes in a deep flameproof casserole. When evenly colored, pour off fat and add onion; cover and cook over moderately low heat until onion is soft.

Moisten bird with the port, simmer until liquid is reduced by half, stir in the paprika and cook 2–3 minutes. Add stock and bouquet garni and season lightly. Cover casserole and cook gently on top of the stove or in a moderate oven (350°F) for $1\frac{1}{2}$ hours or until duck is tender.

Remove duck from casserole and keep hot; discard the bouquet garni. Skim fat from pan.

For sauce: mix flour to a smooth paste with 1 tablespoon liquid from the pan, return this to the remaining liquid and stir over moderate heat until boiling. Simmer 5 minutes, add tomatoes and olives, reheat and taste for seasoning.

Divide duck into 4 portions, arrange on a hot platter and spoon over the sauce. Garnish with parsley. Serve with green peas or beans and very tiny roast potatoes.

Duck Chasseur

5 lb duck
4 tablespoons butter
2 stalks of celery, sliced
1 medium onion, sliced
1 tablespoon flour
$\frac{3}{4}$ cup white wine, or cider
2 cups stock
2 teaspoons tomato paste
bouquet garni
1 cup ($\frac{1}{4}$ lb) mushrooms, quartered
2 tablespoons butter
6–8 small frankfurters, or chipolata sausages

Method

Brown duck for 10–15 minutes in 2 tablespoons butter in a large flameproof casserole. Remove duck and discard all but 1 tablespoon fat. Add celery and onion to casserole and cook until brown. Stir in flour, brown lightly and add wine or cider, stock, tomato paste and bouquet garni. Bring to a boil and simmer 5 minutes.

Cut duck into 4 pieces, replace in casserole, cover and cook over low heat on top of stove or in a moderate oven (350°F) for 45–50 minutes, or until cooked.

Take out duck pieces and arrange on a platter. Strain sauce, discard excess fat and boil to reduce until glossy. Sauté mushrooms in 2 tablespoons butter and add to sauce. Sauté frankfurters lightly in same pan, halving or slicing if large. Spoon sauce over duck and arrange frankfurters along one side.

Braised duck with tomato and olives is garnished with parsley

Cutting up and carving a duck or goose

A Small or Medium Duck or Goose
For a small bird, the same method is used to cut up before or during the cooking process, and to carve the bird, after cooking. The only difference is that, when carving, a fork is used to hold the bird in place instead of using your hand as shown in the drawings.

The pieces are two wings and two legs, with a piece of breast attached to each portion.

A Large Duck or Goose
If a large bird is to be cut up before or during cooking, follow the method for smaller birds. If it is to be carved after cooking, follow the diagrams on the right.

To serve: arrange legs at one end of a hot platter, wings at the other end and pieces of breast in the center. Spoon over a little gravy or sauce.

Poultry shears: specially designed poultry shears are a great help when cutting up all kinds of birds. They should be robustly made with a spring to force the handles apart and a cut out semicircle at the base of one blade to crack around bones. Often the blades are saw-edged, with a slight curve.

Cutting up a duck or goose

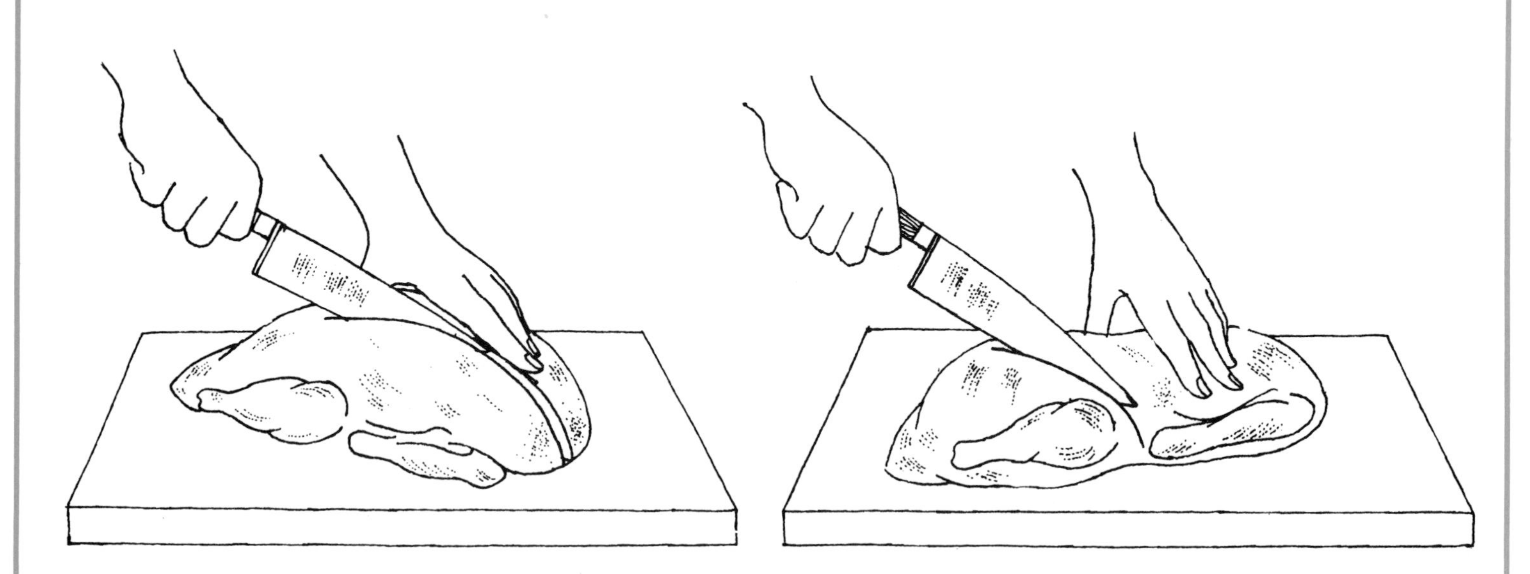

Set the bird on a board; cut along the breastbone. With shears cut through breastbone and each side of backbone, then discard the backbone

Lay each half on board and cut diagonally between wing and leg to separate them. This will give four portions each with some breast. Trim away any bone

Carving a duck or goose

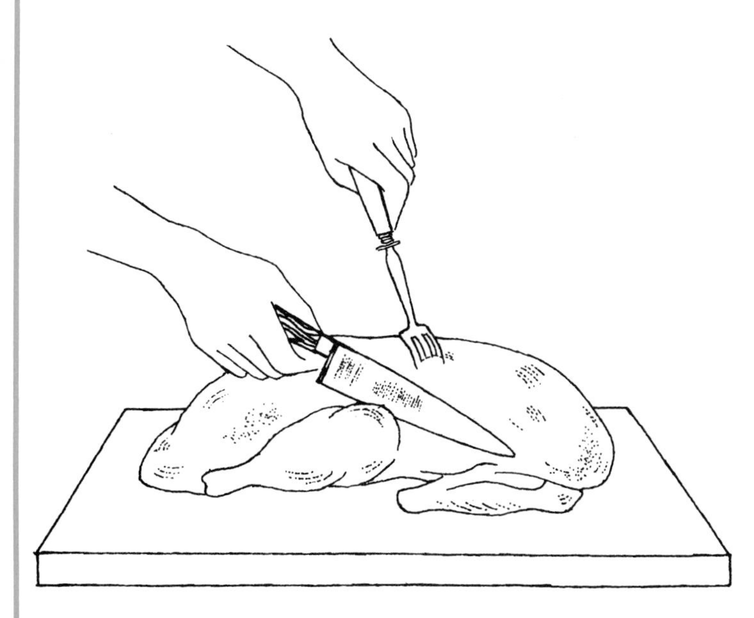

Set the bird on a board and cut off the legs, remembering that, unlike a chicken, the joints are set under the back. Cut legs in half through the thigh joint or slice meat from the bone

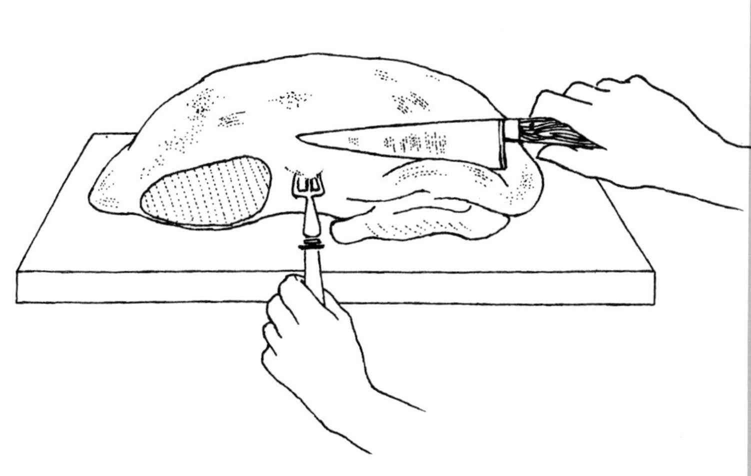

Slip a knife between breastbone and breast to loosen meat. Remove knife. Sever wing joint, angling the knife so that a good piece of the breast meat is left attached to each wing

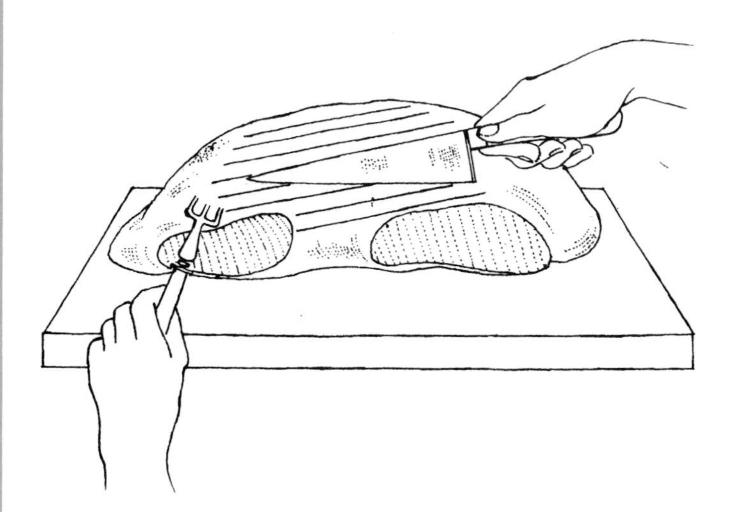

To slice the breast, make the first cut along the breastbone, then make parallel cuts to it down the breast, always slanting the knife well towards the inside of the bird as you slice

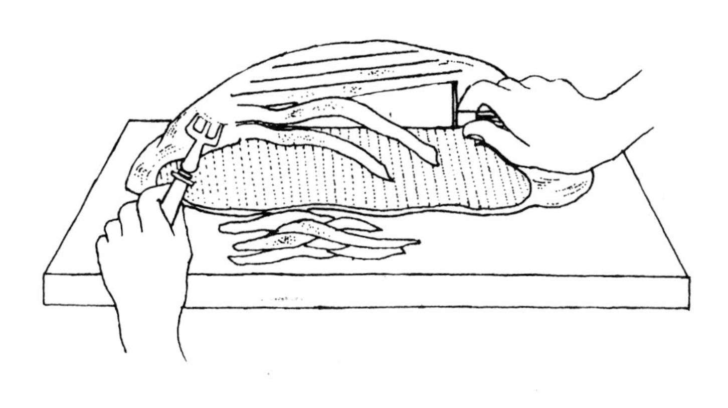

To loosen the slices from the breast of the bird, return the knife along the first cut, then cut firmly up towards the breastbone. This will give good-looking, long slices of meat

Roast Goose

Roast stuffed goose is ready to serve with accompaniments

Roast Stuffed Goose

1 young goose, about 8 lb
2 tablespoons butter
½ teaspoon salt
¼ teaspoon pepper
¼ teaspoon ground ginger
¼ cup port
1½ cups stock, made from goose giblets
1 teaspoon cornstarch mixed to a paste with 1 tablespoon water (optional)

For potato stuffing
3 medium onions, finely chopped
4 large potatoes, peeled and cut in large pieces
½ cup butter, or heavy cream
1½ teaspoons sage
salt and pepper

For garnish
¼ cup butter
10 small tart apples, peeled and cored
¼ cup red currant jelly
2 tablespoons red wine vinegar

Method
To make the stuffing: cover onions with cold water, bring to a boil and simmer 5 minutes, or until tender. Drain well. Boil potatoes in salted water 15–20 minutes until soft, drain and return to pan. Dry over very low heat for 5 minutes, shaking occasionally. Mash with a potato masher or fork, then add butter or cream, beating until potatoes are light. Take from heat and stir in onions and sage and season well.

Set oven at moderately hot (375°F). Fill body of goose with stuffing and truss, sewing each end firmly. Cream the 2 tablespoons butter with seasoning and ginger and spread over breast of bird. Set in a roasting pan and roast in preheated oven for about 2½ hours, basting and turning bird from time to time so it browns evenly. After 2 hours, pour off all fat in roasting pan, spoon the port over goose and continue cooking until skin is crisp.

For the garnish: melt butter in a small roasting pan or shallow flameproof baking dish. Put in apples, baste them well with butter and bake in the same oven as the goose for 40 minutes, or until golden-brown. Put red currant jelly in a pan with vinegar and melt over gentle heat.

Take out goose, remove trussing strings and wing pinion bones and set on a hot platter. Arrange apples around and spoon melted jelly over them. Skim any fat from juices in roasting pan, add stock and boil well to dissolve juices. Adjust seasoning and thicken, if you like, by stirring the cornstarch mixture into the roasting pan, bringing to a boil, stirring, and simmering 1 minute. Strain into a gravy boat. Serve goose with roast potatoes and braised cabbage or Brussels sprouts, or turnips with onions or baked apples with apricot.

Stuffings for Roast Goose

Sauerkraut Stuffing

4 cups fresh or canned sauerkraut
1 tablespoon oil
1 onion, chopped
1 clove of garlic, crushed
1 tart apple, peeled and chopped
2 tablespoons sugar
6–8 juniper berries, crushed (optional)
salt and pepper

Method
Drain fresh sauerkraut and soak it in cold water for 15 minutes, or wash canned sauerkraut. Squeeze out water with your hands and pull sauerkraut apart into shreds to prevent lumps from forming.

In a skillet, fry onion in oil until soft. Add onion to sauerkraut with garlic, apple, sugar and juniper berries, if used, and season well.

Sweet Potato and Celery Stuffing

4 cups cooked, mashed sweet potatoes
5–6 stalks of celery, chopped
2 tablespoons oil
1 onion, chopped
2 cups fresh white breadcrumbs
1 teaspoon sage, salt and pepper

Method
In a skillet, heat oil and fry onion and celery until soft. Stir celery mixture into sweet potatoes with breadcrumbs, sage, salt and pepper.

Turnips with Onions

6–8 small white turnips
3 medium onions, sliced
¼ cup butter
salt
black pepper, freshly ground

Method
Peel and cut turnips in ¼ inch slices. Cook in boiling salted water for 10–15 minutes or until just tender, and drain. Cook onions in butter over medium heat until lightly browned, add to turnips with seasoning and mix gently.

Baked Apples with Apricot

6–8 medium-sized apples
3 tablespoons apricot jam
¼ cup dark brown sugar
grated rind and juice of 1 large lemon
3 tablespoons butter

Method
Set oven at moderately hot (375°F).

Wipe apples, core and pare about ½ inch of peel from top of each. Mix together sugar, lemon rind and juice and butter and pack into apple cavities. Set in a baking dish, pour in just enough hot water to cover the bottom and bake in heated oven for 25–30 minutes or until tender.

Cool slightly, then carefully scoop out about 1 tablespoon of the soft apple pulp, taking care not to break the skins. Mix pulp with apricot jam and add extra sugar and lemon juice to taste if needed. Fill apples with this mixture and reheat to serve.

Zucchini with shrimps is coated with mornay sauce and browned in the oven *(recipe is on page 94)*

SIMPLE DISHES ADD UP TO ELEGANCE

Simple elegance is the keynote of this dinner menu, that starts with zucchini and shrimps in a mornay sauce. Most of the menu can be completely prepared before the guests arrive. Just follow the Timetable on page 94.

To drink with the chicken, try one of the red wines from St. Emilion, a district near Pomerol in eastern Bordeaux. These wines are especially favored by Americans because of their light body and firm flavor. A somewhat softer red wine is the California Ruby Cabernet, made from a strain of the St. Emilion grapes.

Zucchini with Shrimps

Chicken Mojibi (Cold Roast)

Pistachio Rice Salad

Green Salad

Angel Cake with Strawberries

Red wine – St. Emilion (Bordeaux)
or Ruby Cabernet (California)

TIMETABLE

Day before
Roast chicken, cover and refrigerate.
Shell and split pistachio nuts.
Make angel cake and store in airtight tin.
Make syrup for strawberries and store in covered jar.

Morning
Boil rice, drain and dry, set aside in covered bowl.
Blanch zucchini, make filling and fill them. Coat with sauce, cover and chill and leave ready for reheating in heatproof gratin or baking dish.
Carve chicken, arrange pieces and coat with aspic. Chill.
Wash lettuce, etc. For green salad and keep in plastic bag in the refrigerator.
Make vinaigrette dressing for both salads.
Assemble equipment for final cooking from 6:00 p.m. (or before guests arrive) for dinner around 8:00 p.m.

Order of Work

6:00
Whip cream, fill and decorate cake; chill.
Slice strawberries and chill in syrup.
Mix rice salad, cover and chill.

7:30
Set oven at 425°F.

7:45
Put zucchini in oven to heat and brown.
Garnish chicken with watercress.

8:00
Serve appetizer.
Toss green salad just before serving.

You will find that **cooking times** given in the individual recipes for these dishes have sometimes been adapted in the timetable to help you when cooking and serving this menu as a party meal.

Appetizer

Zucchini with Shrimps

8 small zucchini
4 medium tomatoes, peeled, seeded and chopped
2 tablespoons butter
1 shallot, or scallion, finely chopped
1 teaspoon paprika
salt and pepper
½ lb cooked, peeled small shrimps
2 tablespoons grated Parmesan cheese (for topping)

For mornay sauce
2 tablespoons butter
2 tablespoons flour
1¼ cups milk
¼ cup grated Parmesan cheese
½ teaspoon Dijon-style mustard

Method
Wash zucchini and trim each end but do not peel. Blanch by boiling whole in salted water for 5 minutes, draining and refreshing in cold water. Cut a thin lengthwise slice from each zucchini, carefully scoop out flesh with point of a teaspoon, and chop it.

Melt butter in a saucepan, add shallot and cook, covered, over low heat until soft but not brown; add paprika, chopped zucchini flesh and tomatoes. Season with salt and pepper and cook briskly for 2–3 minutes. Stir in the shrimps. Arrange zucchini cases in a buttered oval gratin or baking dish and fill with tomato and shrimp mixture.

For mornay sauce: melt butter in a saucepan, stir in flour and, when foaming, remove from heat and stir in the milk. Bring to a boil, stirring, until sauce thickens. Simmer 2–3 minutes, take from heat, stir in the cheese and mustard. Season to taste and reheat, if necessary, without boiling.

Spoon mornay sauce over the zucchini; sprinkle with cheese and bake in a hot oven (425°F) for 10 minutes or until brown.

To refresh: if green vegetables are drained immediately after they are blanched or cooked, and then 'refreshed' under running cold water, they will retain a bright color.

Above: carefully scoop out flesh of cooked zucchini with the point of a teaspoon

Below: fill zucchini cases before spooning over mornay sauce and browning in oven (see finished dish, page 92)

Entrée

Cold Roast Chicken Mojibi

$3\frac{1}{2}$–4 lb roasting chicken
3–4 tablespoons butter
sprig of fresh rosemary, or 1 teaspoon dried rosemary
salt and pepper
$1\frac{1}{2}$ cups stock, made from chicken giblets
bunch of watercress (for garnish)

For aspic
1 envelope gelatin
2 cans consommé
2 tablespoons brandy (optional)

Trussing needle and string

Note: recipe for true aspic will be given in a future Volume.

Method

Set oven at hot (400°F). Rub chicken with butter; put 1 tablespoon butter inside bird with rosemary and seasoning and truss it (see page 20). Place bird in a roasting pan with half the stock, cover with foil and bake in preheated oven for $1\frac{1}{4}$ hours or until tender, basting from time to time. Chicken should be well browned on all sides.

Watchpoint: to brown evenly and keep good shape, start cooking with the bird lying on its back. After first basting, i.e. after cooking for about 20 minutes, turn bird on its side. When well colored, turn it over, baste again and continue cooking. Finish cooking with breast up.

Remove bird and cool it. Add remaining stock to juices in pan and bring to a boil over direct heat. Taste for seasoning and strain through cheesecloth into a small bowl. Chill and remove all fat from top.

When the chicken is cold, carve it and arrange pieces on a platter; the jelled cooking juices may be spooned between the pieces if you like. Chill.

For aspic, sprinkle gelatin over $\frac{1}{2}$ cup consommé in a small pan. Leave 5 minutes or until spongy; then dissolve over pan of hot water. Stir into remaining consommé, add brandy and stir over a pan of ice water. When aspic is on the point of setting, spoon it quickly over chicken to coat it. Chill, but do not allow it to become too cold or the aspic will crystallize. Just before serving, garnish with watercress. Serve with pistachio rice salad and your favorite green salad.

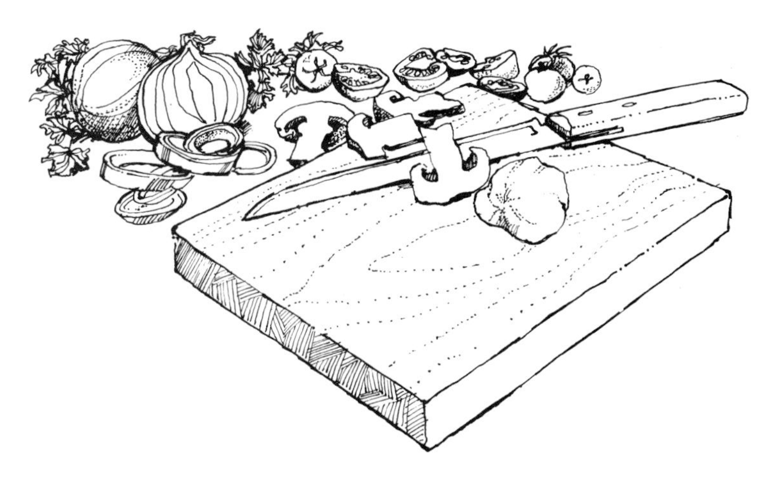

Pistachio Rice Salad

$1\frac{1}{4}$ cups long grain rice
$\frac{1}{2}$ cup shelled pistachio nuts, or 1 cup unshelled nuts
$\frac{1}{2}$ cup currants, or raisins

For vinaigrette dressing
6 tablespoons oil
2 tablespoons vinegar
$\frac{1}{4}$ teaspoon ground cinnamon
salt and pepper

Method

Cook rice in plenty of boiling salted water for 10–12 minutes or until just tender, drain and rinse it thoroughly with hot water. Drain again, then turn onto a large, flat platter and leave to dry. Shell the pistachios, if necessary, and split them.

Make vinaigrette dressing by whisking all the ingredients with salt and pepper to taste, until combined. Mix rice, pistachios and currants and moisten with the dressing, adding more salt and pepper if needed.

Far left: turn the chicken after the first basting
Left: arrange the cooked chicken pieces on a platter before chilling and coating them with aspic

Pistachio nuts are valued in cooking for their sweet, delicate flavor and for their bright green color. Some have a red skin (those with red shells have been dyed) and others have natural skins and shells. They can be combined with pork in stuffings and terrines and are used for decorating pastries. Pistachio-flavored ice cream is also popular.

In some specialty stores, it is possible to find shelled pistachios, but if you shell your own they will have more flavor.

To shell, insert the pointed end of a half shell into the open end of a nut; twist the half shell to force the nut open.

Note: instructions for making a green salad, and for carving a chicken were given on pages 22 and 21 respectively.

Cold chicken Mojibi is garnished with watercress and served with pistachio rice salad

Dessert

Angel Cake with Strawberries

$\frac{3}{4}$ cup cake flour
$1\frac{1}{4}$ cups sugar
1 cup egg whites (about 6 large eggs)
$\frac{1}{4}$ teaspoon salt
1 teaspoon cream of tartar
$\frac{1}{4}$ teaspoon almond extract
1 teaspoon vanilla

To finish
$1\frac{1}{2}$ cups heavy cream
1 tablespoon sugar
1 teaspoon vanilla
box of strawberries

For syrup
$\frac{1}{2}$ cup sugar
$\frac{1}{2}$ cup water
2 tablespoons brandy, or 1 teaspoon vanilla

8–9 inch tube pan; pastry bag; medium star tube

Method

Set oven at moderately hot (375°F). Sift flour 3 times with $\frac{3}{4}$ cup of the sugar. In a large bowl, beat egg whites with salt until foamy; add cream of tartar and beat until whites stand in a stiff peak. Add remaining sugar, 2 tablespoons at a time, beating between each addition until glossy. Add almond extract and vanilla with last addition of sugar. Sift flour and sugar mixture over egg whites, $\frac{1}{4}$ cup at a time and fold in lightly with metal spoon.

Gently spoon mixture into an ungreased pan. Level the surface and draw a knife through the mixture to break any air bubbles. Bake in preheated oven for 30–35 minutes or until cake springs back when the top is pressed gently with a fingertip.

Invert pan over a wire rack to cool, making sure that top of cake does not touch rack (use a funnel or bottle as a stand if the pan has no legs). When cold, loosen sides of cake with a spatula and turn out. Cut in three layers with a serrated-edged knife.

Watchpoint: a serrated-edge knife is important as cake's texture is delicate – use a gentle sawing motion for best results.

Whip the cream until it holds a soft shape, add sugar and vanilla and continue whipping until stiff. Spread each layer of cake with cream, reshape cake and coat completely with whipped cream. Fill a pastry bag fitted with a star tube with remaining cream and pipe rosettes on top and sides of cake. Decorate with whole, unhulled strawberries.

Hull remaining strawberries, then cut in thick slices. For syrup, dissolve sugar in water over low heat, bring to a boil and cook 2 minutes. Chill, stir in brandy or vanilla and pour over strawberries in a glass bowl; serve separately.

Below: angel cake with more strawberries, soaked in syrup, to serve separately

Draw knife through cake mixture to break up air bubbles

COOKING FOR THE WEEKEND

Everyone is eager to celebrate the holiday season with a weekend away from home. If you are expecting guests, remember that the secret of successful entertaining is advance planning, which includes the kitchen as well as the rest of the house. If you prepare as much as possible before guests arrive, you will be able to enjoy their company all the more, knowing that only a minimum of work will be needed to produce a series of perfectly co-ordinated meals.

Start at the beginning of the week by planning the menus, and do the marketing well ahead, first making a list so that nothing is forgotten. Then prepare as much as you can two, or even three, days in advance. The following work plan will show how you can produce four easy but interesting meals, plus a special treat for Sunday breakfast.

Try soft-cooked eggs, hot cross buns (recipe is on page 101) and coffee for a weekend breakfast

WORK PLAN

SATURDAY LUNCH

Tuna Quiche
Cheese and Fresh Fruit

SATURDAY DINNER

Zucchini with Shrimps
Cold Chicken Mojibi
Pistachio Rice Salad
Green Salad
Angel Cake
with Strawberries
(see menu, pages 92–97)

SUNDAY BREAKFAST

Soft-cooked
Eggs
Hot Cross Buns
Coffee

SUNDAY LUNCH

Boiled Ham
with Carrots and Onions
Creamed Potatoes
Coffee and
Walnut Galette

Two or Three Days Ahead

1 Make angel cake and store in airtight tin (if necessary, make double quantity for Sunday's trifle).

2 Make syrup for strawberries and store in screw-top jar.

3 Make meringues for galette and store in airtight tin.

Friday

1 Make pastry for tuna quiche, line pan and bake blind, keeping excess for hot cross buns.

2 Make filling and complete quiche. Cover and refrigerate ready for baking.

3 Roast chicken. Cool, cover and refrigerate. Dissolve juices in roasting pan, strain, cover and chill.

4 Make coffee filling for galette, but do not add cream; cover tightly.

5 Make hot cross bun dough, let rise and shape it. Cover buns and refrigerate at once. Alternatively, bake buns completely; store in an airtight tin.

6 Cook ham with vegetables for Sunday lunch and refrigerate, covered.

Saturday Morning

1 Carve chicken for dinner, arrange on platter with jellied juices and chill.

2 Make aspic and coat the chicken.

3 Blanch zucchini, make filling, fill, then cover and chill.

4 Boil rice for salad and prepare other salad ingredients. Wash enough lettuce for Saturday and Sunday evenings, pat dry and store in plastic bag.

5 Make dressing for rice and green salads and cover.

6 Bake tuna quiche for lunch.

Saturday Evening

See Timetable on page 94.

Sunday Morning

1 For breakfast, bake or reheat hot cross buns; cook eggs, make coffee.

2 For lunch, scrape or peel potatoes and cook them; make white sauce, spoon over potatoes and keep hot in top of double boiler.

3 Reheat ham.

4 Whip cream and complete galette, filling it with coffee cream. Chill.

5 Drain ham and carve. Drain vegetables, reserving liquid for soup, and arrange on platter.

6 Add parsley to potatoes and serve.

SUNDAY DINNER

Soup of the Day
Ham, Chicken or Mushroom Omelet
Green Salad
Fruit Trifle

Sunday Evening

1 Make soup with leftovers of green salad, ham liquid and cooked vegetables.

2 Make trifle with leftovers from angel cake and strawberries in syrup or use ladyfingers and fruit suggested in recipe.

3 Make omelets using chicken or ham left from Saturday dinner and Sunday lunch, or sautéed fresh mushroom slices.

4 Toss washed lettuce with remaining dressing and serve.

SATURDAY LUNCH

Tuna Quiche

For rich pie pastry
2 cups flour
$\frac{1}{2}$ teaspoon salt
$\frac{1}{2}$ cup butter
2 tablespoons shortening
1 egg yolk
3–4 tablespoons cold water

For filling
1 can ($6\frac{1}{2}$ oz) tuna, flaked
4 medium tomatoes, peeled, halved and seeded
3 tablespoons butter
3 medium onions, finely sliced
2 tablespoons flour
1 cup milk
salt and pepper
grated nutmeg to taste
3 eggs, beaten to mix
$\frac{1}{4}$ cup grated Parmesan or Gruyère cheese

Deep 9 inch pie pan

Method
Prepare pie pastry and chill 30 minutes. Roll out, line pie pan and bake blind in a hot oven (400°F) for 15 minutes or until pastry is set but not quite brown. Remove from oven and reduce heat to 350°F.

In a saucepan, melt butter, add onions, and cook over low heat until soft. Stir in flour, add milk and stir this sauce until it thickens and boils. Simmer 2 minutes. Take from heat, add seasoning and nutmeg to taste and the beaten eggs. Arrange tomatoes and tuna in bottom of pie shell and pour in sauce. Scatter with grated cheese and bake in heated oven (350°F) for 30 minutes or until set and brown. Serve hot or cold.

SUNDAY BREAKFAST

Hot Cross Buns

4 cups flour
$\frac{1}{2}$ teaspoon salt
pinch each of cinnamon, allspice, nutmeg and cloves
1 cup milk
1 cake compressed, or 1 package dry yeast
6–8 tablespoons butter
$\frac{1}{4}$ cup sugar
2 eggs, slightly beaten
1 cup currants, or raisins
2 tablespoons finely chopped candied peel (optional)
little extra flour (for sprinkling)
pie pastry (for decoration)
$\frac{1}{4}$ cup milk mixed with 1 tablespoon sugar (for brushing)

These buns are an Easter specialty but are good at any time of year.

Method
Sift flour with salt and spices into a warm bowl. Heat milk to lukewarm and sprinkle over yeast and add butter. Stand in a warm place for 5 minutes or until yeast is dissolved and butter melted, stirring occasionally. Stir in sugar and eggs. Make a well in flour, add liquid ingredients, and beat hard until smooth.

Turn dough onto a floured board, work in currants or raisins and candied peel, and knead dough with hand for 5 minutes, or until it is smooth and elastic. (Kneading is done by pushing the dough away from you with heel of the hand and drawing it back with the fingers.) Place dough in a warm, greased bowl, sprinkle surface lightly with flour, cover with a damp towel and leave to rise in a warm place for $1\frac{1}{2}$ hours or until dough has doubled in bulk. Punch out air with your fist, work dough 1 minute, cover and let rise again in a warm place for 30 minutes more.

Shape dough into small round buns the size of a biscuit and place on a greased baking sheet. Mark a cross on the top of each bun with a knife and cover each cut with 2 thin strips of pie pastry. (If this is not available, make a stiff paste with 1 cup flour and enough water to bind.) If not baking immediately, cover with plastic wrap and refrigerate at once. Set oven at hot (425°F).

Leave buns to rise in a warm place for 15 minutes or until almost double their size (if buns are not baked immediately, they may rise sufficiently in the refrigerator). Brush tops with sweetened milk and bake in heated oven for 15 minutes or until buns sound hollow when tapped. Serve hot or cool.

Note: a steamy atmosphere in the oven is best for baking buns; to create this, put a roasting pan of boiling water in the bottom of the oven.

SUNDAY LUNCH

Boiled Ham with Carrots and Onions

3 lb piece country ham (without bone)
6 peppercorns
1 bay leaf
8 medium carrots, peeled
8 small white onions, peeled

Method

If the ham is cured with a great deal of salt, soak it in cold water for 3–4 hours, then drain.

In a flameproof casserole, cover ham with cold water, bring slowly to a boil and skim surface of liquid well. Add peppercorns and bay leaf, cover and simmer 1 hour. Then add whole carrots and onions and continue simmering $\frac{1}{2}$ hour or until vegetables and ham are tender. Let stand 15 minutes, then drain ham and carve it in even slices. Arrange meat with vegetables on a warm platter. (Reserve the cooking liquid to make soup for supper unless it is very salty.)

If preparing ham in advance, cook a slightly shorter time and leave ham and vegetables in liquid ready to reheat. Serve creamed potatoes separately.

Creamed Potatoes

10–12 small new potatoes, scrubbed or pared
2 tablespoons chopped parsley

For white sauce
3 tablespoons butter
3 tablespoons flour
2 cups milk
salt and pepper

Method

Put potatoes in boiling salted water, cover and cook 15 minutes or until they are just tender when pierced with a pointed knife. Drain. For the sauce, melt butter in a saucepan, stir in flour and, when foaming, take pan from heat and stir in milk. Bring to a boil, stirring, simmer 2 minutes and season to taste. Add potatoes and reheat carefully without boiling. Stir in parsley just before serving.

If preparing potatoes in advance, keep hot or reheat them in the top of a double boiler.

Coffee and Walnut Galette

4 egg whites
1 cup sugar
1 cup walnut halves
granulated, or confectioners' sugar (for sprinkling)
1 cup heavy cream, whipped until it holds a soft shape

For filling
2 cups strong black coffee
$2\frac{1}{2}$ tablespoons cornstarch
$\frac{1}{4}$ cup sugar
1 teaspoon vanilla

2 baking sheets covered with non-stick silicone paper; pastry bag; $\frac{1}{2}$ inch plain tube (optional)

Method

Set oven at very low (250°F).

Beat egg whites until they hold a firm peak but are not dry. Add 1 tablespoon sugar and continue beating until mixture is glossy. With a metal spoon, fold in remaining sugar to make meringue mixture. Draw an 8 inch diameter circle on the silicone paper and spread this area thickly with meringue. Shape the remaining meringue mixture into very small circles on the second paper-lined sheet, preferably forcing it through a pastry bag fitted with the plain tube. Place a walnut half on top of each small circle and sprinkle all the tops with sugar.

Put the large round on a shelf in the center of the oven and the small meringues on a shelf beneath. Bake 1 hour or until crisp and lightly browned, reversing the shelves halfway through cooking. Peel away the paper carefully and cool meringues on a wire rack.

To make filling, mix cornstarch with $\frac{1}{2}$ cup coffee and bring remaining coffee to a boil with the sugar. Take from heat and stir in cornstarch mixture. Return to heat and cook, stirring until thick. Cook 2 minutes, take from heat, stir in vanilla, cover and cool. Stir from time to time while cooling to prevent lumps from forming. Chop remaining walnuts.

To assemble galette, just before serving, use a little whipped cream to stick small meringues onto edge of large round and fold the rest into the coffee mixture. Pile coffee filling in center and scatter with chopped walnuts.

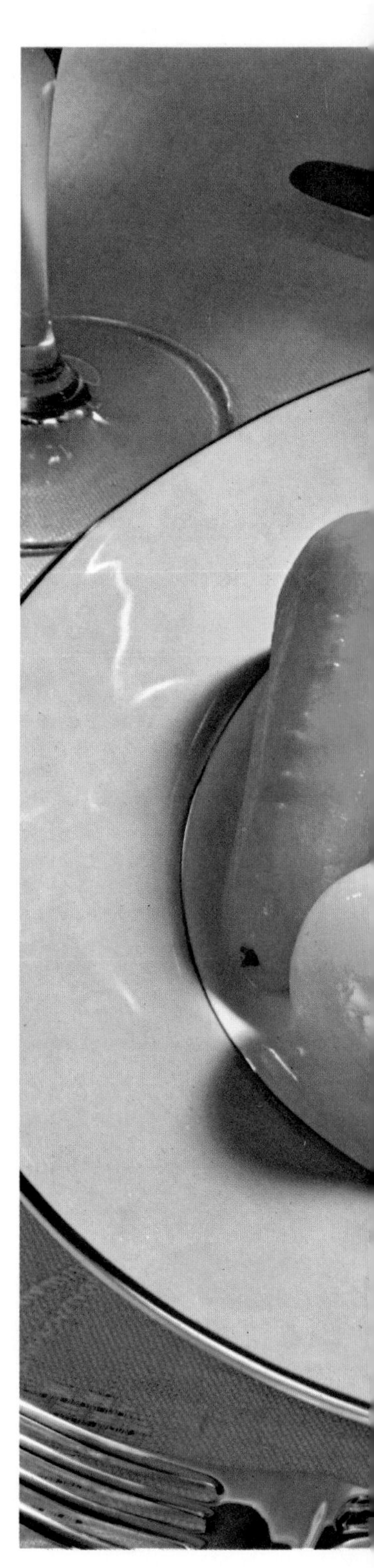

SUNDAY DINNER

Soup of the Day

2 tablespoons butter
1 medium onion, finely chopped
leftover green salad (with its dressing), chopped
$1\frac{1}{2}$–2 cups leftover cooked vegetables (potatoes in white sauce, or carrots and onions from ham), coarsely chopped
2 cups liquid from cooking ham (if very salty, use bouillon instead)
2 cups milk
salt and pepper

Do not throw out leftover green salad – it cannot be served again because the dressing wilts the leaves after a few hours, but with the addition of a little milk or stock it makes delicious soup. The dressing gives it an unusual tang.

Method

In a large pan, melt butter and sauté onion until soft. Add leftover salad and continue cooking, covered, over very low heat for 10 minutes. Add vegetables to pan with ham liquid and simmer 10 minutes more. Purée in a blender or work through a food mill. Return to pan with the milk, bring just to a boil and taste for seasoning.

Boiled ham, cooked with its own vegetables and served with creamed potatoes, makes an easy-to-prepare lunch

Fruit Trifle

1 package ladyfingers, or equivalent in leftover angel cake
2 cups fresh, or canned, fruit, including leftover strawberries
$\frac{1}{4}$ cup raspberry jam
$\frac{3}{4}$ cup heavy cream, stiffly whipped

For custard
$1\frac{1}{2}$ tablespoons cornstarch
2 cups milk
$\frac{1}{4}$ cup sugar
1 teaspoon vanilla
3 egg yolks, beaten to mix

Method

Spread ladyfingers or large cubes of cake with raspberry jam and place in the bottom of a glass bowl. Drain fruit and spoon $\frac{1}{2}$ cup juice over the cake (if fresh fruit has no juice, use orange juice). Spread the fruit on top. For custard, mix cornstarch with $\frac{1}{4}$ cup milk. Heat remaining milk with the sugar and, when boiling, stir in cornstarch, off the heat. Cook the mixture, stirring constantly, until it thickens and simmer 2 minutes. Take from heat and beat in vanilla with egg yolks. Pour custard over fruit in bowl and chill until set. Just before serving, spread stiffly whipped cream over the custard.

The English dessert of **trifle** isn't a 'trifle' at all. The basic recipe is a luscious combination of cream, custard, fruit and cake, often flavored with sherry, but there are many variations. The 19th century cookbook author, Mrs. Beeton, listed no fewer than a dozen.

A slice of marble cake (recipe is on page 117) shows the marbled effect of the light and dark cake batters

HOW TO BAKE CAKES

Cakes have a reputation of being tricky, but careful preparation is the key to success. Flavor, texture and appearance of a cake depend almost entirely on the ingredients and the way they are combined before the cake is put in the oven.

Flavor and texture are governed by the choice and preparation of the correct ingredients – a reliable recipe has been tested again and again to find exactly the right balance and you cannot expect to get good results if you do not follow it exactly—for instance you cannot substitute regular flour for cake flour or corn syrup for honey simply because you don't have the right item on hand.

Mix ingredients thoroughly, particularly in the early stages. When instructions say 'cream butter and sugar until light and fluffy' it means just that; if you don't beat long enough, the cake will be heavy and may have an uncooked streak or layer.

Appearance depends mainly on correct preparation of the cake pan – any sugar or flour coating must be spread evenly and bumps must be smoothed from a paper lining – and on careful baking. Uneven or incorrect oven heat is almost invariably the reason for a cake scorching or rising unevenly.

Preparation of ingredients

Flour should always be sifted with a good pinch of salt before use; this aerates the flour and removes any small lumps; the salt improves the flavor.

Fats are important to the success of any cake and different kinds give different results. Butter is perfect for baking because it gives an incomparable flavor and improves the keeping properties of the cake, but margarine, which is easier to cream, can be used in place of butter in almost all recipes.

Shortening is excellent for cakes where the proportion of sugar and liquid in the recipe is large. Shortening is a vegetable fat and, if stored properly, keeps many months.

Sugars are very important and the wrong type can completely ruin a cake. Granulated sugar must be used for creamed cake mixtures. If the sugar is not beaten in properly, the cake will have a spotted top.

Light brown sugar is good for dessert and fruit cakes, while dark brown sugar is used for rich fruit and Christmas cakes to improve the flavor. Some recipes may substitute a combination of granulated sugar and molasses for dark brown sugar.

Confectioners' sugar gives a fine, close texture to cakes and pastry. It lumps easily and should always be sifted before using.

Eggs are essential for a light cake. They expand and set on heating and so trap any air that is beaten into the mixture. For maximum volume, allow eggs to reach room temperature before whipping or adding them to a cake. When called for in recipes, an egg is assumed to be 2 oz or graded 'large'.

Nuts and candied fruits. When using nuts, check the recipe to see if they should be shredded, slivered or chopped. This seemingly small variation has a decided effect on flavor, texture and appearance, particularly when the nuts are used to top the cake.

If possible, buy candied fruit in 'caps' or large pieces rather than chopped, as these large pieces are softer and richer in flavor. Scoop out the sugar from the center and shred the peel on a coarse grater – the fine slivers look attractive in a finished cake.

Leavening agents. Baking powder is a commercial preparation made of acid and alkali – usually cream of tartar and bicarbonate of soda (baking soda). It should be sifted with flour in the proportions given in the recipe.

Bicarbonate of soda mixed with an acid ingredient such as sour milk, buttermilk, vinegar or molasses has a similar effect to baking powder and these combinations are often used in quick breads and coffee cakes. Small quantities of soda with vinegar or molasses may be added to help fruit cakes rise.

Do not store self-rising flour or baking powder for too long as they deteriorate, particularly in a damp atmosphere.

For high altitude baking, where smaller quantities of leavening agents are needed, use specially-tested recipes.

Baking

Prepare cake pans before mixing is begun. They are usually brushed evenly with melted butter, margarine or shortening and then sprinkled with flour and/or sugar, according to the recipe. Some recipes suggest lining the base of the pan with a circle of wax or silicone paper, but this is not necessary for creamed and sponge cakes if the pan has a loose base. Pans for rich fruit cakes should always be lined.

Preparing the Oven

The next step is to set the oven and arrange the shelves. It is vital to set the cake in the right position as well as to bake it at the right temperature. There must be room for the heat to circulate in the oven around baking sheets and cake pans, otherwise the cakes will bake unevenly.

Once in the oven, do not move a cake until the mixture is set and avoid opening the oven door until the minimum time given in the recipe is reached. This minimum is a rough guide to baking time but you should always test a cake before removing it from the oven.

Testing a Cake

Creamed cake mixtures should spring back when pressed lightly with a fingertip. Test fruit, and some creamed, cakes by piercing the center with a fine skewer, which should come away clean. All cakes start to shrink from the sides of the pan when they are done. Before baking, read about ovens and oven temperatures on page 127.

Methods of Mixing

Rubbing in: used for muffins and some quick breads. Fat is cut into sifted flour, then rubbed lightly with fingertips until mixture resembles fine breadcrumbs. Muffins and quick breads are at their best when eaten fresh or within 1 day of baking.

Warming: suited to spice cakes, gingerbread and some fruit cakes. A variety of leavening agents can be used with this method and, as a general rule, the cake is moist and close in texture and the flavor improves with keeping.

Fat, sugar and liquids are melted in a saucepan before being added to flour. The mixture before baking (cake batter) is much thinner than in regular mixtures and is easily poured into the prepared pan.

Creaming: used for most rich cakes. It gives a light, even-textured cake with a soft, slightly moist top which should be smooth and fairly flat.

For best results follow these rules: have butter or margarine and eggs at room temperature (about 70°F); mixture will be easier to beat and less likely to curdle.

Beat the butter (or fat) until it is soft and creamy.

Beat sugar a little at a time into the well-creamed butter, scraping the sides of the bowl once or twice during this process. Any sugar crystals left on the sides of the bowl will give finished cake a speckled top.

When the butter and sugar look like whipped cream, the eggs may be added. If the amount of sugar is *under* 1 cup, the eggs should be beaten together and added a little at a time. If using *more* than 1 cup sugar, eggs may be added individually. Beat very well after each addition of egg.

Watchpoint: curdling is most likely to happen at this stage. It is caused either because the butter (or fat) and sugar have not been thoroughly creamed or because the eggs are too cold. Curdling can be corrected by standing the mixing bowl in a little hot water and beating vigorously. If, however, you still have more egg to add, stir in 1 tablespoon of sifted flour with the addition of each egg.

Then, using a metal spoon, gently fold in flour and any liquid given in recipe. At this point do not beat or stir as this will remove air from mixture and make cake rise and crack.

Walnut layer cake – see recipe on page 115

EQUIPMENT FOR CAKE-MAKING

You can easily make your first cake with nothing other than a cake pan and the general equipment like bowls and spoons listed on opposite page. However, the more ambitious your baking efforts become, the more specialized equipment you will covet.

The first major item is certain to be an electric mixer, or at least a hand-held electric beater so you avoid the hard work of creaming butter and beating eggs. Then come all the different sizes and shapes of cake pans. Whether a cake be sponge, fruit or muffin, the recipe will call for a particular pan, and baking times and results can be quite different if another one is substituted.

The standard sizes of cake pans are listed below but you will find literally dozens of others in specialty kitchen stores. Many of them, like Mickey Mouse faces and Valentine hearts, are gimmicks and, like tiered wedding cake pans, are rarely used.

French and European gâteaux should be baked in a pan with sloping sides called a 'moule à manqué'. When the cake is decorated, icing flows easily down the sides giving a smooth, even finish.

For most regular cakes you can get by with 8–9 inch diameter layer cake pans, a couple of square loaf pans and a 9–10 inch diameter tube pan. Springform pans are not essential, although you may have problems without one for cakes such as cheesecakes that are hard to turn out. Add to these a dozen muffin tins and you are well equipped.

When it comes to pastry, this Cooking Course often calls for metal pie pans with a fluted edge and removable base so that the finished pie can be completely unmolded and slid onto a platter for serving. Flan rings are an alternative – plain circles of metal 1 inch or so high which are set on a baking sheet so the pastry shell can be lined and cooked inside. When done, the ring is lifted from the pie, that is then transferred to a platter. You will also need a dozen small plain or fluted tartlet pans.

Flan rings and pie pans need no preparation as pastry contains enough fat to prevent a pie shell from sticking. With cakes it is a different matter. Depending on the recipe, cake pans must be brushed with a thin layer of melted butter, margarine or shortening, or rubbed evenly with any of these fats. Some recipes, particularly sponges, then call for the pan to be coated with flour and/or granulated sugar. Sprinkle 1–2 tablespoons into the pan, shake until evenly coated all over and turn out the excess.

As with all kitchen equipment, cheap baking items are a false economy for they will buckle in the heat and give you scorched, misshapen results – this applies particularly to baking sheets, which can twist so much they spill their contents in the oven. Nonstick pans are well worth their extra cost.

The following is a list of cake-making equipment generally available – build up a stock gradually.

General Equipment

Baking sheets
Cookie cutters, plain and fluted
Electric, or rotary, beater
Flat wooden spoon or wooden spatula, or wire whisk
Flour sifter
Foil
Metal spoons
Pastry bag and various tubes, e.g. plain, star and shell, $\frac{1}{4}$, $\frac{1}{2}$ and $\frac{3}{8}$ inch diameters
Rubber spatula
Sugar thermometer
Wax paper
Wire racks

Cake Pans

Boat molds
Flan rings, 8, 9, 10 and 12 inch diameters
Jelly roll pan, 10 X 15 inches
Kugelhopf (fluted ring) mold
Layer cake pans, 7, 8 and 9 inch diameters
Loaf pans: large (9 X 5 X 3 inches) or medium (8$\frac{1}{2}$ X 4$\frac{1}{2}$ X 2$\frac{1}{2}$ inches)
Madeleine molds
Moule à manqué, 8, 9 and 10 inch diameters
Muffin pans
Pie pans, 7, 8, 9, 10, 12 and 14 inch diameters
Rectangular cookie pan, 7 X 11 inches
Savarin (plain ring) mold
Springform pans, 7, 8 and 9 inch diameters
Square pans, 8 and 9 inch
Tartlet pans
Tube pans, 9 and 10 inch diameters

Tools for Cake-making

Like most skills, cake-making is easier if you use the right tools.

Flat wooden spoon or wooden spatula is best for creaming butter and beating stiff mixtures like egg yolks and sugar or butter and sugar. If a regular wooden spoon is used, the mixture tends to collect in the bowl of the spoon and is not worked properly.

Wire whisk can be used for the same tasks, but be sure it is spotlessly clean or it will impart a metallic flavor to the mixture.

Rubber spatula can easily scrape the last spoonful of mixture from the bowl.

Metal spoon with a long handle is correct for folding – the metal cuts cleanly into a mixture and so combines ingredients more quickly.

Rotary beater is necessary for light mixtures like egg whites or whole eggs and sugar which should have as much air as possible beaten into them.

Electric mixer beats as well or better than you can by hand. Adjust the speed of the mixer according to the consistency of mixture and the amount of air you want to incorporate.

To Line a Round Cake Pan

1 Cut a circle of wax or silicone paper the diameter of pan base. Cut a strip of paper about 1 inch longer than circumference of pan and 2 inches more than the depth.
2 Make a fold along one long edge of a strip and cut slits in fold about $\frac{1}{2}$ inch deep and 1 inch apart.
3 Press strip around sides of pan so folded cut edge overlaps pan base.
4 Place circle of paper inside over base of pan to hold overlap in place. Brush with a little melted shortening or butter to prevent cake from sticking.

A springform cake pan makes unmolding easier – unbuckle the side and slide it away from the cake. This pan usually has two interchangeable bottoms – one with a tube as shown here, and one flat

Pound cake has been split and is then sandwiched with jam

Pound Cake

$\frac{3}{4}$ cup butter
$\frac{3}{4}$ cup sugar
3 eggs
$1\frac{1}{2}$ cups cake flour
pinch of salt
1 teaspoon baking powder
1 teaspoon vanilla
1–2 tablespoons milk
confectioners' sugar (for sprinkling)

8 inch springform cake pan, or 9 inch tube pan

Pound cake is so called because it is made with equal weights of butter, sugar, eggs and flour. It can be flavored with grated orange or lemon rind, with nuts and dried or candied fruits, or it can be split and sandwiched with frosting or jam.

Method

Grease cake pan and line bottom with wax paper. Set oven at moderate (350°F).

Use the creaming method: cream butter thoroughly in a large bowl, add sugar very gradually and beat until mixture is soft and light. Beat eggs until frothy, add a little at a time to the sugar mixture, beating thoroughly after each addition. Sift flour with salt and baking powder and fold into the batter in three portions, alternately with vanilla and enough milk to make the mixture drop easily from the spoon. Spread the mixture in the prepared pan and bake in preheated oven for 45 minutes or until done.

To test if cake is ready: it should spring back when pressed lightly with a fingertip. The top will be golden-brown and the sides slightly pulled away from the pan. Cool 5 minutes. Have 2 wire racks ready; put a folded clean dish towel or a double thickness of paper towel on one of them. Loosen the sides of the cake with a small spatula, place the rack with the towel or paper on top of the cake (towel next to cake) and turn over; remove the pan and paper lining from the cake. Place second rack on top of cake base and carefully and quickly turn it over again. This prevents the cake from having the marks of the cake rack on top.

When cake is cool, leave plain or split and fill with jam or frosting; sprinkle top generously with confectioners' sugar.

Grandmother's Pound Cake

1 cup butter
1 cup dark brown sugar
4 eggs, separated
3 tablespoons sherry, brandy or rum
2 cups flour
pinch of salt
$\frac{1}{4}$ teaspoon ground allspice
$\frac{1}{4}$ teaspoon ground cinnamon
$\frac{1}{2}$ teaspoon ground nutmeg
$1\frac{1}{2}$ cups currants
$1\frac{1}{2}$ cups raisins
$1\frac{1}{2}$ cups golden raisins
$\frac{1}{2}$ cup slivered almonds
$\frac{1}{3}$ cup finely chopped mixed candied peel

8 inch springform pan

Method

Set oven at moderately low (325°F). Line the cake pan with a double thickness of wax paper and grease it (see box on page 109).

Cream the butter, gradually beat in the brown sugar and continue beating until the mixture is soft and fluffy. Beat in the egg yolks, one by one, with the sherry, brandy or rum.

Sift the flour with the salt and spices and divide it into three. Fold one portion into the butter mixture. Toss the second portion with the dried fruits, almonds and candied fruits. Then beat the egg whites until they hold a stiff peak.

Stir the fruit and flour mixtures into the butter mixture, then stir in the remaining portion of flour with the egg whites.

Spoon the mixture into the prepared pan and bake in the heated oven for $2\frac{1}{2}$ hours or until a skewer inserted in the center comes out clean. If the cake is brown after about $1\frac{1}{2}$ hours' baking, cover with a sheet of foil.

Cool the cake in the pan for 30 minutes, then turn out onto a wire rack to cool completely. Store the cake in an airtight container – it mellows if kept for about 2 weeks.

English Madeleines

$\frac{2}{3}$ quantity pound cake mixture, made with $\frac{1}{2}$ cup butter, $\frac{1}{2}$ cup sugar, 2 eggs, 1 cup cake flour, $\frac{3}{4}$ teaspoon baking powder, $\frac{3}{4}$ teaspoon vanilla and 1 tablespoon milk
$\frac{1}{4}$ cup apricot, or red currant, glaze
6 tablespoons shredded coconut
8 candied cherries

14–16 dariole molds, or small muffin pans

Method

Set oven at moderately hot (375°F), thoroughly grease and lightly flour the molds or pans.

Prepare pound cake mixture and fill molds or pans half full. Bake in preheated oven for 8–10 minutes, or until golden-brown and top springs back if pressed with a fingertip. Turn out onto a wire rack and cool.

Trim cake tops to give them a flat surface when inverted and turn them upside down. Spear each on a fork for easy handling, brush with warm apricot or red currant glaze, roll immediately in coconut and top with half a cherry.

Welsh Cheese Cakes or Tartlets

1 cup quantity of rich pie pastry **(see page 49)**

For filling
$\frac{1}{3}$ quantity pound cake mixture, made with $\frac{1}{4}$ cup butter, $\frac{1}{4}$ cup sugar, 1 egg, $\frac{1}{2}$ cup cake flour, $\frac{1}{3}$ teaspoon baking powder, $\frac{1}{3}$ teaspoon vanilla, and $\frac{1}{2}$ tablespoon milk
1–2 tablespoons jam
granulated sugar (for sprinkling)

12 tartlet pans

Although known as cheese cakes or tartlets, these have nothing to do with cheese or cheese-cake.

Method

Prepare the pastry dough, roll it thinly and line the pans. Set the oven at hot (400°F).

Put a little jam in each tartlet and prepare the pound cake mixture. Put 1 tablespoon mixture in each pastry case, and bake in preheated oven for 20 minutes or until golden-brown. Cool slightly, turn from the pans onto a wire rack. Serve hot or cold and sprinkle with sugar just before serving.

Raisin and Walnut Cake

1 lb raisins
2 cups chopped walnuts
$\frac{1}{4}$ cup brandy
$1\frac{1}{2}$ cups all-purpose flour
$\frac{1}{2}$ cup self-rising flour
pinch of salt
1 cup butter
1 cup dark brown sugar
4 eggs
$\frac{3}{4}$ cup candied cherries, halved

Savarin or ring mold (5–6 cup capacity)

Method

Put raisins in an airtight container with the brandy and let stand overnight.

Set oven at moderate (350°F). Grease and flour the mold and sprinkle with half the nuts. Sift the flours and salt together. Mix the remaining walnuts with the soaked raisins, candied cherries and about one-third of the flour.

Cream the butter, add the sugar gradually and beat until the mixture is light and fluffy. Beat in the eggs, one at a time, and fold in half of the remaining flour. Add the fruit mixture, then fold in the remaining flour.

Spoon the mixture into the prepared mold and bake in the heated oven for about $1-1\frac{1}{4}$ hours or until a skewer inserted in the cake comes out clean. Let cool in the pan for 10 minutes, then turn out onto a wire rack to cool completely.

Coconut Cake

2 cups cake flour
2 teaspoons baking powder
$\frac{1}{2}$ teaspoon salt
$\frac{1}{2}$ cup shortening
$1\frac{1}{4}$ cups sugar
3 eggs, well beaten
$\frac{1}{2}$ cup milk
1 teaspoon vanilla
2 cups boiled frosting
1 cup shredded coconut

Two 8 inch cake pans

Method

Set oven at moderate (350°F) and grease and flour cake pans.

Sift flour with baking powder and salt. Cream shortening well, add sugar gradually and beat until the mixture is light and fluffy. Add eggs, a little at a time, beating thoroughly between each addition. Fold in the sifted flour in three portions alternately with milk and vanilla. Spoon mixture into the prepared pans and bake in the preheated oven for 25 minutes or until a fine skewer inserted in the center of the cakes comes out clean. Turn out onto a rack and cool.

Sandwich cakes with boiled frosting and coat top and sides. Before the frosting sets, cover cake thickly with the coconut.

Boiled Frosting

2 cups sugar
1 cup water
pinch of cream of tartar
2 egg whites
1 teaspoon vanilla

Sugar thermometer

Makes 2 cups.

Method

In a saucepan heat sugar and water gently until sugar is dissolved. Dissolve cream of tartar in 1 teaspoon water, add to sugar syrup, cover and bring to a boil. Boil 2 minutes, remove the lid, insert sugar thermometer and boil sugar syrup steadily without stirring to 240°F (soft ball stage). Meanwhile beat egg whites until they hold a stiff peak.

Stop syrup cooking by dipping the base of the pan in cold water. Then, holding the pan well above the egg whites, pour in the hot syrup in a steady stream, beating continuously. Beat until the mixture holds its shape and is no longer glossy. Add vanilla and spread quickly over cake with a palette knife in bold, sweeping strokes, as the frosting sets quickly.

Note: it is possible to make this frosting without a sugar thermometer. After boiling for 8 minutes, test as follows. Lift a little syrup out on a spoon – it should fall to form a thread 3 inches long – or take a small kitchen tool (such as a whisk) that has a rigid ring or loop at the end and dip ring into the boiling syrup. Holding it up blow through ring. If ready, syrup flies away like a bubble.

Madeira Cake

1 cup butter
grated rind of $\frac{1}{2}$ lemon
$1\frac{1}{4}$ cups sugar
5 eggs
$3\frac{1}{4}$ cups all-purpose flour
pinch of salt
2 teaspoons baking powder
1 cup milk
slice of candied citron peel
confectioners' sugar

8 inch springform pan

Method

Set oven at moderate (350°F); grease cake pan and coat with a mixture of flour and granulated sugar.

Cream butter together with lemon rind in a bowl, gradually add sugar and continue beating until the mixture is light and soft. Beat in the eggs, one at a time, adding 2 teaspoons flour with each one. Sift remaining flour with salt and baking powder and fold into sugar mixture in three portions, alternately with milk. Spoon into the prepared pan and bake in the preheated oven for 30 minutes; then place the slice of citron peel on top of the cake. Reduce the heat to moderately low (325°F) and bake 30 minutes longer or until cakes spring back when lightly pressed with a fingertip. Turn out on a wire rack to cool. Before serving, sprinkle with confectioners' sugar.

This recipe may also be baked in two $8\frac{1}{2} \times 4\frac{1}{2} \times 2\frac{1}{2}$ inch loaf pans.

Coconut cake is sandwiched and coated with boiled frosting before adding shredded coconut

Madeira cake is light and lemon-flavored (recipe is on page 112)

Walnut Layer Cake

$2\frac{1}{4}$ cups cake flour
3 teaspoons baking powder
$\frac{1}{2}$ teaspoon salt
$\frac{3}{4}$ cup shortening
$1\frac{1}{2}$ cups sugar
1 cup milk
1 teaspoon vanilla
4 egg whites

To finish
2 cups boiled frosting
$\frac{1}{4}$ cup chopped walnuts
8 walnut halves

Three 8 inch cake pans

Method
Set oven at moderate (350°F) and grease and flour the cake pans.

Sift flour with baking powder and salt. Cream shortening thoroughly. Beat in sugar gradually and continue beating until very light and soft. Stir in flour alternately with milk and vanilla. Beat egg whites until they hold a stiff peak, and fold into the cake mixture in three portions. Divide the mixture evenly between the three prepared pans, and bake in heated oven for 30 minutes or until cake springs back when pressed lightly with a fingertip.

Turn out onto a wire rack and cool. Combine $\frac{1}{2}$ cup frosting with the chopped walnuts and quickly spread half on one cake layer. Place second layer on top, coat with remaining walnut frosting and cover with final layer. Cover cake with remaining plain frosting and decorate with walnut halves.

Pineapple Layer Cake

Follow the recipe for walnut layer cake, bake and allow it to cool. Prepare the same quantity of frosting, but combine $\frac{1}{3}$ cup with 3 tablespoons canned, crushed pineapple, drained. Spread this between the layers of cake, cover the top and sides with remaining frosting and decorate with slices of candied pineapple.

Cherry Layer Cake

Follow the recipe for walnut layer cake and divide the mixture as before into three; color one portion a delicate pink with red coloring. Pour into pans, bake and cool.

Prepare boiled frosting, but reserve one-third of the mixture. Into this fold $\frac{1}{2}$ cup maraschino cherries, drained and halved. Sandwich the layers with this filling, putting the pink layer in the center, and cover the top and sides with the remaining plain frosting.

Devil's Food Cake

$1\frac{1}{2}$ cups all-purpose flour
$\frac{1}{4}$ teaspoon baking powder
1 teaspoon baking soda
pinch of salt
$\frac{1}{2}$ cup cocoa
1 cup cold water
$\frac{1}{2}$ cup shortening
$1\frac{1}{4}$ cups sugar
2 eggs

Two 8 inch cake pans

Method
Set oven at moderate (350°F) and grease and flour the cake pans.

Sift flour with baking powder, baking soda and salt. Blend cocoa with water. Cream shortening thoroughly, gradually add sugar and beat until the mixture is light and fluffy. Whisk eggs until frothy and add to the sugar mixture a little at a time, beating well after each addition. Fold in the sifted flour in three portions alternately with water and cocoa mixture. Spoon into the prepared pans and bake in preheated oven for 30 minutes or until a fine skewer comes out clean when inserted into the center of the cakes. Turn out onto a wire rack and cool.

Sandwich the cakes with chocolate fudge frosting, then cover completely with frosting.

Right: for devil's food cake, mix fudge frosting while the cake cools (see finished cake on next page)

Chocolate Fudge Frosting

2 cups sugar
1 cup water
1 tablespoon corn syrup
$\frac{1}{4}$ cup butter
$\frac{1}{2}$ cup cocoa

Sugar thermometer

Method
Place all ingredients in a large saucepan, stir them to mix, then dissolve sugar over gentle heat without stirring. Insert sugar thermometer, bring to a boil and cook to 240°F on the sugar thermometer.

Take pan from heat and cool to lukewarm without stirring. Beat until the frosting holds its shape.

Watchpoint: to prevent possible sticking during boiling draw a wooden spoon through the mixture from time to time, but never stir continuously as this can cause the frosting to 'grain' or crystallize.

Devil's food cake is sandwiched and completely covered with the chocolate fudge frosting

Caramel Cake

$1\frac{1}{2}$ cups sugar
$\frac{1}{2}$ cup hot black coffee, or water
2 cups cake flour
$\frac{1}{2}$ teaspoon salt
3 teaspoons baking powder
$\frac{1}{2}$ cup shortening
2 eggs, well beaten

Two 8 inch cake pans

Method

Set oven at moderate (350°F): grease and flour the cake pans.

Place $\frac{1}{2}$ cup sugar in a small heavy pan and melt it over gentle heat without stirring. Cook steadily to a rich brown caramel, take from heat and immerse base of pan in water. At once pour in the hot coffee or water.

Watchpoint: Stand back as the mixture will sputter.

Return to low heat and stir to dissolve the caramel. Pour mixture into a measuring cup, cool and add cold water to make $\frac{1}{2}$ cup.

Sift flour with salt and baking powder; cream shortening thoroughly and gradually beat in remaining sugar. Beat until light and fluffy, then add eggs a little at a time, beating between each addition. Fold in flour in three portions, alternately with the caramel mixture and spoon into the prepared cake pans.

Bake in preheated oven for 25 minutes or until cake springs back when lightly pressed with a fingertip. Turn out onto wire rack and cool. Sandwich the cakes and coat them with caramel icing.

Caramel Icing

6 tablespoons butter
5 tablespoons light cream
2 tablespoons granulated sugar
3 cups confectioners' sugar, sifted

Method

Heat butter with cream until melted. In a small heavy pan, melt granulated sugar over gentle heat and cook to a deep brown caramel. Take from heat and carefully add butter and light cream, stirring until all caramel is dissolved.

Stir in confectioners' sugar and beat until icing is smooth, creamy and spreads easily.

Mocha Frosting

$\frac{1}{4}$ cup butter
3 tablespoons cocoa
$\frac{1}{4}$ teaspoon salt
1 teaspoon vanilla
$\frac{1}{4}$ cup boiling water
1 teaspoon instant coffee
2 cups confectioners' sugar, sifted

Makes about 2 cups.

Method

Cream butter thoroughly and stir in cocoa, salt and vanilla. Mix water with coffee until dissolved. Beat sugar and coffee liquid alternately into butter mixture until smooth.

Marble Cake

$4\frac{1}{2}$ cups cake flour
2 teaspoons baking powder
$\frac{1}{2}$ teaspoon salt
1 cup shortening
1 teaspoon vanilla
1 cup sugar
$\frac{1}{2}$ cup milk
1 teaspoon baking soda
1 teaspoon cinnamon
1 teaspoon cloves
1 teaspoon nutmeg
1 cup dark brown sugar, firmly packed
4 eggs, separated
$\frac{1}{2}$ cup molasses
1 cup buttermilk

10 inch tube pan

Method

For white batter: sift $2\frac{1}{2}$ cups of the cake flour with baking powder and $\frac{1}{4}$ teaspoon salt. Cream $\frac{1}{2}$ cup shortening thoroughly with vanilla. Gradually add sugar and beat until light and fluffy. Stir in flour mixture in three portions, alternately with milk. Reserve.

For dark batter: sift remaining flour with baking soda, remaining salt and spices. Thoroughly cream remaining shortening. Gradually add brown sugar and beat until light and soft. Beat in egg yolks one by one together with molasses. Stir in flour mixture in three portions, alternately with buttermilk. Beat egg whites until they hold a soft peak; fold into white batter.

Place $\frac{1}{2}$ cup white batter in greased tube pan, then $\frac{1}{2}$ cup dark batter next to it. Continue alternating batters until all is used. Bake in a moderate oven (350°F) for 1 hour or until top springs back when pressed lightly with a fingertip. Cool, loosen with a spatula and turn out onto a cake rack. When cold, coat with mocha frosting.

Applesauce Cake

$\frac{3}{4}$ cup apple sauce
$\frac{1}{2}$ cup coarsely chopped walnuts
1 cup raisins
2 cups flour
1 teaspoon baking powder
$\frac{1}{4}$ teaspoon ground cinnamon
$\frac{1}{4}$ teaspoon ground nutmeg
$\frac{1}{4}$ teaspoon ground cloves
$\frac{1}{4}$ teaspoon ground allspice
1 teaspoon salt
6 tablespoons shortening
$1\frac{1}{3}$ cups sugar
1 egg
confectioners' sugar (for sprinkling)
heavy cream, stiffly whipped or vanilla ice cream (to serve)

8 inch round or square cake pan

Method

Set oven at moderate (350°F) and grease pan.

Sift flour with baking powder, spices and salt. Cream the shortening, beat in sugar as thoroughly as possible and beat in the egg. Stir in the apple sauce, then fold in the flour, walnuts and raisins. Spoon mixture into the prepared pan and bake in heated oven for 45–50 minutes or until a skewer or toothpick inserted in the center comes out clean. Cool until lukewarm in the pan, then turn out onto a wire rack to cool completely. Sprinkle with confectioners' sugar and serve whipped cream or vanilla ice cream separately.

Applesauce cake – serve with whipped cream or vanilla ice cream, if you wish (recipe is on page 117)

Lemon wine cookies are topped with icing and sprinkled with chopped pistachios (recipe is on page 121)

Brownies should have crusty tops and rich, crumbly centers

Brownies

2 squares (2 oz) unsweetened chocolate
$\frac{1}{2}$ cup butter
1 cup sugar
2 eggs
$\frac{1}{2}$ cup flour
pinch of salt
1 cup coarsely chopped pecans
$\frac{1}{2}$ teaspoon vanilla

8 inch square pan

Makes 16, 2 inch brownies.

Method
Set oven at moderate (350°F) and grease the pan.

Melt chocolate in a pan over hot water. Cream butter until soft; gradually add sugar and beat until mixture is light and fluffy. Add eggs, one at a time, beating after each addition. Sift flour with salt and stir into mixture. Stir in nuts, melted chocolate and vanilla.

Spread mixture in the prepared pan and bake in preheated oven for 25–30 minutes or until a dull crust has formed. Cool slightly and cut into squares.

Butterscotch Brownies

$\frac{1}{4}$ cup butter
1 cup dark brown sugar
1 egg
1 teaspoon vanilla
$\frac{1}{2}$ cup flour
$\frac{1}{2}$ teaspoon salt
1 teaspoon baking powder
$\frac{3}{4}$ cup shredded coconut, or chopped dates (optional)

Cake pan (11 X 7 inches)

Makes 12, $1\frac{1}{2}$ X $3\frac{1}{2}$ inch brownies.

Method
Set oven at moderate (350°F) and grease the cake pan.

In a saucepan, melt butter, stir in sugar and heat until melted. Cool slightly and beat in egg and vanilla. Sift flour with salt and baking powder and stir into the butter mixture. Stir in coconut or dates. Spread mixture in the prepared pan and bake in preheated oven for 25 minutes or until a crust has formed. Cool slightly before cutting into bars or squares while still in pan.

Lemon Wine Cookies

2 cups flour
pinch of salt
$\frac{1}{2}$ cup shortening
$\frac{1}{3}$ cup sugar
grated rind of 1 lemon
2 egg yolks
1 tablespoon sherry

For topping
1 cup confectioners' sugar
1–2 tablespoons lemon juice
1 tablespoon chopped pistachios

3 inch plain cookie cutter

If you prefer, a $\frac{1}{2}$ tablespoon lemon juice and $\frac{1}{2}$ tablespoon water may be substituted for the sherry in this recipe. Makes 24 cookies.

Method
Set oven at moderate (350°F).

Sift flour with salt into a bowl. Rub in shortening with the fingertips until the mixture resembles crumbs. Stir in sugar and grated lemon rind. Mix egg yolks with the sherry, add to the lemon mixture and knead dough lightly with the hand until smooth.

On a floured board, roll out the dough $\frac{1}{8}$ inch thick and cut out 3 inch rounds with the cookie cutter. Set the rounds on a greased baking sheet and bake in heated oven for 8–10 minutes or until cookies are just beginning to brown. Transfer them to a wire rack to cool.

To make icing for topping: sift confectioners' sugar into a small bowl and stir in enough lemon juice to make a stiff paste. Set the bowl over a pan of hot water and warm the icing until tepid. It should thinly coat the back of a spoon. If it is too thin, beat in more sifted confectioners' sugar.

Coat cookies with icing and sprinkle a few chopped pistachios in the center of each.

Icebox Cookies

These are a boon to busy cooks who have to feed a large family or guests at short notice. Make a large batch of dough, shape and freeze it in foil or wax paper for use later. (It keeps in refrigerator for up to a week.) The mixture is very soft, so do not try to shape it into a roll until it has been well chilled. Never add extra flour to make handling easier as this spoils texture of finished cookies.

Icebox Cookie Variations
Add to the recipe for vanilla icebox cookies $\frac{1}{2}$ cup chopped nuts, or $\frac{1}{2}$ cup chopped raisins, or $\frac{1}{4}$ teaspoon each of ground cinnamon, allspice and cloves, or 2 oz sweet chocolate, melted.

Vanilla Icebox Cookies

$1\frac{3}{4}$ cups all-purpose flour
pinch of salt
2 teaspoons baking powder
$\frac{1}{2}$ cup butter
1 cup sugar
1 egg, slightly beaten
1 teaspoon vanilla
$\frac{1}{2}$ teaspoon grated lemon rind (optional)

Makes about 40 cookies.

Method
Sift flour with salt and baking powder. Cream butter thoroughly, gradually add sugar and beat until light. Beat in the egg, add vanilla and grated lemon rind, if desired, and stir in the sifted dry ingredients. Chill mixture one hour or until firm enough to handle and shape into long rolls 2 inches in diameter. Roll in wax paper or foil and chill at least 24 hours, or freeze. Cut in very thin slices and bake on a greased baking sheet in a preheated hot oven (400°F) for 8–10 minutes or until lightly browned.

Butterscotch Icebox Cookies

Follow above recipe but substitute dark brown sugar for granulated used there.

TYPES OF FLOUR

Flour is one of the most important staple foods and there are an amazing number of types available, each with different properties in cooking. Quite apart from the wheat types, flour can be made from grains like rice and oats, from roots like arrowroot and even from beans and nuts. The following are the most common types in general use.

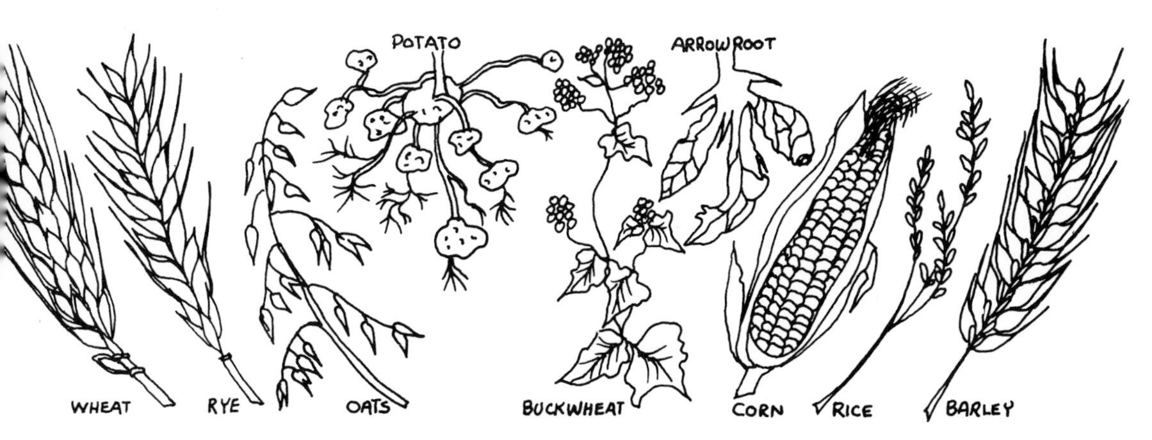

How to Measure Flour

Many older cookbooks call for flour to be sifted before measuring but today flour millers and cooks have at last reached an agreement and flour, no matter what type, is *never* sifted before it is measured.

To measure flour, choose a measure of correct size with a flush rim for leveling. Fill it to overflowing, spooning flour directly from package. Do not bang measure on table; level top with a knife or spatula.

For cakes, tip the flour straight from the measure into a sifter or a fine strainer and sift it onto a sheet of waxed paper. Any dry ingredients like salt and baking powder should be sifted with flour. For very light cakes like angel cake, the flour may be sifted 2–3 times.

Wholewheat or graham flour

As its name implies, this flour is milled from the whole wheat grain. It is neither refined nor bleached, and is generally used in yeast breads or close-textured quick breads and muffins.

Regular or all-purpose flour

Available bleached or unbleached, and most widely used. If a recipe calls for 'flour' (in pastry, cakes, breads, cookies or sauces), use all-purpose flour unless otherwise stated.

Cake flour

Highly refined, bleached wheat flour used mainly in cakes to give a light, open texture.

Self-rising flour

Regular flour to which the usual quantities of leavening agents and salt have been added for convenience. Do not keep it for more than 6 months (less in a damp atmosphere) as the leavening agents deteriorate on standing.

Enriched flour

Refined and bleached flour has had vitamins and minerals removed. Enriching puts these back – so that enriched flour approximates the vitamin and mineral content of wholewheat flour. Most all-purpose flour is also enriched.

Wheat germ

The vitamin and mineral-rich kernel of the wheat grain. Not, strictly speaking, a flour, it is added to mixtures containing other types of flour, to enrich them.

Instant flour

A slightly granular flour which needs no sifting and does not cause lumps in sauces. However, it reacts differently from regular flour, so never use it as a substitute but keep to recipes specially created for it.

Semolina flour

A high gluten flour made from hard wheat. It is used in all commercial pastas, making them firm and easy to handle. You can find semolina in a few Italian stores for making pasta at home.

Cracked wheat or bulgur

Whole grains of wheat milled to varying degrees of coarseness. It is used in Greek and Middle Eastern cooking to make pilaf and occasionally added to bread.

Bran

The outer layer of the wheat grain which is added to other flours for muffins, breads, etc.

Oat flour and oatmeal

Flours of varying consistencies made of oat grains. They give a hearty flavor and texture to breads and cookies.

Rye flour

Made from rye grain, this flour gives a close, moist texture to breads and usually is mixed with wheat flour.

Buckwheat flour

Buckwheat is not, strictly speaking, a cereal grain but the seed of a herb native to central Asia. It adds flavor and a coarse texture to muffins, waffles, pancakes, and authentic Russian blini pancakes.

Corn meal

Coarsely ground, dried corn which is used in the traditional corn and spoon breads of the South. It can be yellow or white, according to the type of corn.

Cornstarch

Made from starchy part of corn grain. Used mainly as a thickener, it gives a clear mixture when cooked, unlike flour.

Arrowroot

A fine, white flour made from the root of a tropical plant. It, too, is often used to thicken sauces and has a lighter, less sticky effect than cornstarch.

Potato flour or starch

Used mainly in kosher cooking potato flour is also favored by French chefs for thickening particularly delicate sauces.

Rice flour

A dry, starchy flour, sometimes used in cakes or moist mixtures like macaroons. Do not confuse it with waxy rice flour, milled from different kinds of rice, used as a stabilizer in commercial sauces and soups.

COOKING EQUIPMENT

The list on the right details the equipment needed in your kitchen if you want to try the recipes included in the full Grand Diplôme Course. It also gives you an idea of how to equip a kitchen from scratch. The list is not meant to be comprehensive, nor are all the items absolutely essential.

You may already possess suitable alternatives to some of the things mentioned and, in any case, you will not need them all immediately. However, you will find from experience that using the right equipment saves time and usually produces the best results. Sizes recommended have been chosen for their general usefulness; you may want to change them to suit your style of cooking and size of household. Electric appliances are invaluable in the kitchen, but they are a luxury and you can do without any of them. First choice should be a blender, which saves endless time and gives cream soups a consistency impossible to achieve by hand. Otherwise, take your pick – if you like to bake you will want an electric mixer or, if your tastes incline to savory dishes, you may prefer an electric carving knife or a grinder.

Only one rule to remember – you'll find it cheaper in the end to buy the best equipment you can afford. A well-stocked kitchen will give lasting pleasure; cheap tools wear out quickly and are inefficient to use.

Cooking Equipment

Beater: rotary or electric

Bowls: mixing bowls,
10–12 inch diameters
3 bowls of varying sizes, from 5 inch diameter (quart capacity)

Brushes: pastry brush (a 1 inch paint brush is best)
vegetable brush

Carborundum (fine steel): for sharpening knives

Chopping board, wooden

Colander

Containers: for leftovers
for freezer storage

Emery paper, fine: for cleaning carbon steel knives

Foil

Food mill

Fork, with carving guard

Gloves: rubber gloves
oven gloves, or pot holders

Grater

Grinder

Juicer: for lemons and other fruit

Knives: French chefs' knives are of carbon or stainless steel. Carbon stays sharper, but must be kept scrupulously clean
bread knife – with serrated edge
chopping knife – with a 7 inch pointed blade
filleting knife – with a 6 inch flexible, narrow pointed blade
palette knife – or spatula, with about a 7 inch blade
fruit/vegetable knife – stainless steel, serrated-edge, with a 3–4 inch-pointed blade (carbon steel will stain some fruits and vegetables)
vegetable knife – with a 3–4 inch blade

Ladle

Measures: heatproof quart measure
set of U.S. standard measuring spoons
set of U.S. standard cup measures

Needles: larding needle
trussing needle

Openers: bottle opener (corkscrew)
can opener

Paper: wax paper
non-stick (silicone) cooking paper (from which food lifts very easily without sticking). Particularly useful for cake-making and although expensive, can be used more than once

Pastry bag, waterproof: with one medium-sized star tube (for cream and fillings)
3 plain round tubes, $\frac{1}{2}$ inch and $\frac{3}{8}$ and $\frac{1}{4}$ inch (for piping and decoration)

Pepper mill

Plastic bags

Plastic wrap, transparent (or wax paper)

Poultry pins (or meat lacers)

Rolling pin

Scissors, kitchen (preferably with half-hole in blade for cutting poultry)

Skewers: 5–9 inches in length

Slicer, vegetable (or mandoline)

Spatula, rubber or plastic

Sponge

Spoons: 2–3 wooden spoons and spatulas from 9–14 inches in length
1 large metal spoon for basting and stirring
slotted spoon

Strainers: nylon strainer
wire sieve strainer

Towels: dish towel
paper towels

Vegetable peeler

Whisks: small whisk
balloon whisk (for beating egg whites). Ideally this should fit the curve of your mixing bowl

MEASURING & MEASUREMENT

The recipe quantities in the Course are measured in standard level teaspoons, tablespoons and cups and their equivalents are shown right. Any liquid pints and quarts also refer to U.S. standard measures.

When measuring dry ingredients, fill the cup or spoon to overflowing without packing down and level the top with a knife. All the dry ingredients, including flour, should be measured before sifting, although sifting may be called for later in the instructions.

Butter and margarine usually come in measured sticks (1 stick equals $\frac{1}{2}$ cup) and other bulk fats can be measured by displacement. For $\frac{1}{3}$ cup fat, fill the measuring cup $\frac{2}{3}$ full of water. Add fat until the water reaches the 1 cup mark. Drain the cup of water and the fat remaining equals $\frac{1}{3}$ cup.

For liquids, fill the measure to the brim, or to the calibration line.

Often quantities of seasonings cannot be stated exactly, for ingredients vary in the amount they require. The instructions 'add to taste' are literal, for it is impossible to achieve just the right balance of flavors in many dishes without tasting them.

Liquid measure	Volume equivalent
3 teaspoons	1 tablespoon
2 tablespoons	1 fluid oz
4 tablespoons	$\frac{1}{4}$ cup
16 tablespoons	1 cup or 8 fluid oz
2 cups	1 pint
2 pints	1 quart
4 quarts	1 gallon

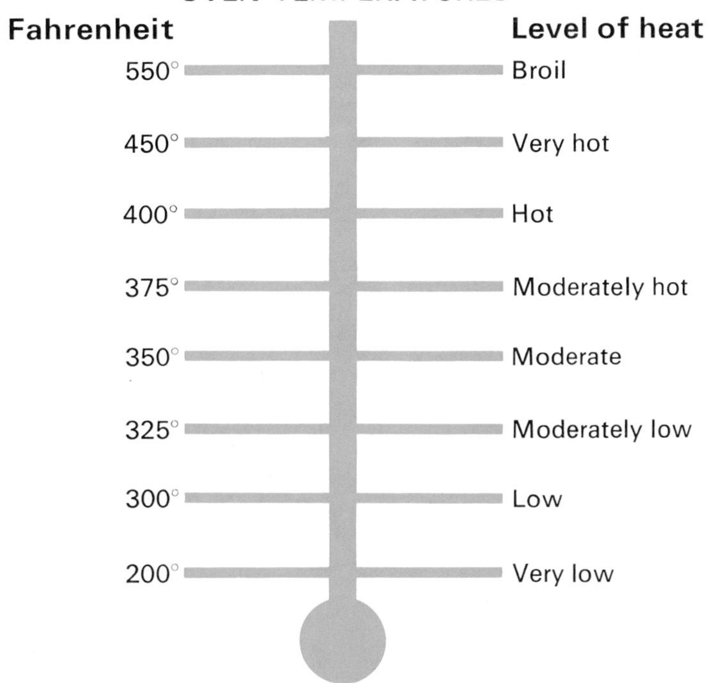

OVEN TEMPERATURES AND SHELF POSITIONS

Throughout the Cooking Course, oven temperatures are stated in degrees Fahrenheit and in generally agreed levels of heat such as 'high' and 'moderate'. The equivalents are shown on the table above.

However, exact temperature varies in different parts of an oven and the thermostat reading refers to the heat in the middle. As the oven temperature at top and bottom can vary as much as 25°F from this setting, the positioning of shelves is very important. In general, heat rises, so the hottest part of the oven is at the top, but consult the manufacturer's handbook about your individual model.

Pans and dishes of food should be placed parallel with burners or elements to avoid scorched edges.

When baking cakes, there must be room for the heat to circulate in the oven around baking sheets and cake pans; otherwise the underside of the cakes will burn. If baking more than one cake in an oven that has back burners or elements, arrange the cakes side by side. If the oven has side burners, arrange cakes back and front.

Oven thermostats are often inaccurate and are unreliable at extremely high or low temperatures. If you do a great deal of baking or question the accuracy of your oven, use a separate oven thermometer as a check on the thermostat.

Glossary of Basic Cooking Terms

When you come across unfamiliar words in this Cooking Course, just refer to this Glossary of basic cooking terms.

Aromatics Ingredients which give flavor and scent to a dish, e.g. herbs, spices, garlic – whether in cooking or added to a cooked dish.

Arrowroot Starch made from the root of a tropical plant, used to thicken sauces. It gives a clearer, less sticky effect than cornstarch; add in the same way but cook only until just boiling.

Aspic Clear gelatin made from clarified chicken/meat/fish stock used with the appropriate dish, e.g. chicken in aspic. Wine/liqueur may be added to stock and, if necessary, powdered gelatin may be used to set it.

Bain Marie See **Water bath.**

Bake To cook by dry heat, e.g. in oven.

Barbecue To broil/roast on a spit/rack, normally over charcoal.

Bard To cover lean meats/game with thinly sliced bacon/pork fat before cooking.
See also **Lardons.**

Baste To spoon hot fat/liquid several times over food as it roasts. Use a large metal spoon or basting bulb.

Beat To stir vigorously with a circular motion using a spoon/whisk to give lightness to a mixture.

Béchamel French name for a white sauce made with milk infused with seasonings and thickened with butter and flour.

Beurre See **Butter.**

Bind To moisten with liquid to keep a mixture together.

Blanch To whiten meats and remove strong flavors from vegetables by immersing in cold water, bringing to a boil, and draining before further cooking. Green vegetables should be put directly into boiling water and cooked for up to 1 minute.

Blanquette Stew of lamb/veal/chicken/rabbit with a rich sauce of cooking stock. Milk/cream and egg yolks are added.

Blend To stir a mixture until it is completely combined and smooth.

Boil To cook (in) water/stock at 212°F when water bubbles vigorously.

Bone To remove all bones from meat/fish/poultry with a small sharp knife.

Bouillon Meat/vegetable stock. If using commercial cans/powder, add less salt when seasoning.

Bouquet garni Traditionally a bunch of parsley, thyme and bay leaf tied with string or in a piece of cheesecloth for flavoring stews and sauces. Other herbs can be added. Remove bouquet garni before serving.

Braise After browning meat in fat/oil, to cook slowly by moist heat in a small amount of liquid, in a tightly covered container. Suited to tougher cuts of meat requiring slow cooking. May be cooked on a bed of sweated, diced vegetables (see **Mirepoix**). To braise vegetables, e.g. celery, first blanch, then shake pan frequently while braising to prevent contents from sticking.

Brine Salt and water solution used in preserving meats, etc.

Broche (à la) Cooked on a spit.

Brochette (en) Small pieces of meat/fish/poultry with vegetables, broiled on a skewer, e.g. kebab.

Broil To cook meat/fish/poultry by direct heat, usually under electric/gas broiler or over charcoal/barbecue fire.

Butter

Beurre blanc: Sauce of butter, white wine/wine vinegar, fish stock, chopped shallots. Served with poached/boiled fish.

Beurre manié (kneaded butter). Liaison of twice as much butter as flour worked together as a paste on a plate with a fork and added in small pieces to thicken a mixture or liquid (usually at end of cooking process).

Beurre noir. Butter (preferably clarified) cooked to deep brown, then sharpened with reduced vinegar/lemon juice. Used mainly for fish/brains. Parsley/capers may be added.

Beurre noisette. Butter (preferably clarified) cooked to a nut-brown color.

Clarified butter: see **Clarify 2.**

C

Caramelize 1 To dissolve sugar slowly in water then boil steadily, without stirring, to a deep honey color. **2** To give a thin caramel topping by sprinkling the surface of dessert with granulated sugar and broiling carefully.

Carbonade Stew, usually of beef, cooked with beer. Literal meaning: to cook over coals.

Casserole Stewpan/Dutch oven. Stews of meat/game/fish/poultry and vegetables cooked in liquid/sauce very slowly in the oven or over heat in a stewpan, are also referred to as casseroles.

Chapon A crust of French or regular bread rubbed with a peeled clove of garlic that is buried in a green salad to impart a light flavor of garlic. After tossing salad in dressing, remove the chapon before serving.

Chill To cool but not to freeze, by putting food in the refrigerator, or over ice.

Chop To cut into small uneven pieces with a sharp knife.

Chowder Soups based on fish or shellfish but may also be made with meat and vegetables. Most fish and seafood chowders have a seasoned milk base, with the fish and vegetables cooked until tender, but not pureed.

Clarify 1 To remove impurities by melting used fat, e.g. beef drippings, with one-third quantity of water, boiling, straining and cooling. When fat is set, scrape any sediment from base of solidified fat. **2** To clarify butter by heating gently until foaming, skimming well, leaving to set to a solid cake; sediment (milk solids) at the bottom is discarded. **3** To clear cold stock with egg whites by whisking while bringing to a boil, cooling and straining.

Compote Fresh/dried fruit poached in a syrup, usually of sugar and water.

Concasser To chop roughly or shred coarsely. Usually applied to tomatoes that have first been peeled, halved, and then very gently squeezed to remove the seeds.

Condiment Seasoning, usually a spice like pepper, a highly flavored sauce, or a relish.

Consistency Degree of thinness/thickness of a mixture, especially important in batters, cake-making, pastry-making and sauces.

Consommé Clear soup made from well flavored meat stock that is concentrated and clarified before serving hot or cold. See **Clarify 3**.

Cool To lower to room temperature.

Cornstarch Very fine flour made from corn, used largely as a thickening agent.

Court bouillon Stock made from water, root vegetables, wine/vinegar, herbs and seasoning for poaching fish/veal and for use in sauces.

Cream To beat a substance, usually a fat, until soft enough almost to fall from the spoon.

Crêpe Very thin French pancake; can be sweet or savory.

Croquette Savory mixture shaped into rounds/balls/cones, coated with egg and breadcrumbs, and fried in deep fat. Usually made of chopped meat/hard-cooked egg/fish bound with thick béchamel sauce; also mashed potatoes.

Croûte Small round or decorative shape of bread, lightly toasted/fried and spread or piled high with a savory mixture. Also used as a garnish. Not to be confused with pie or bread crust (also called croûte in French).

Croûton Small square/dice of fried bread/potato to accompany purée or cream soups.

Curdle Curdling occurs when a smooth mixture separates into solid and liquid parts, often due to the action of heat, or an acid. When possible, recipes state how to rectify this.

Custard Cooked mixture of eggs and milk, usually sweetened.

Deglaze After removing excess fat, to heat stock and/or wine together with sediments left in roasting/frying pan so that gravy/sauce is formed.

Dégorger To remove impurities and strong flavors before cooking. This can be done by: **1** Soaking food, e.g. uncooked ham, in cold water for a specified length of time. **2** Sprinkling sliced vegetables, e.g. cucumber, with salt, covering with a heavy plate, leaving up to 1 hour, washing away salt and pressing out excess liquid with a weighted plate.

Devil To marinate, e.g. in Worcestershire sauce, or to apply a seasoned/spiced paste to meat/fish/poultry before broiling/frying, often in breadcrumbs. A deviled or barbecue sauce can be served separately.

Dice To cut meat/fruit/vegetables into small squares.

Dissolve To melt a solid substance usually by mixing with a liquid, if necessary over heat.

Dough Basic mixture of flour, liquid and fat for bread and pastry.

Dressing See **Stuffing**.

Entrée The main course of a meal, although in France the entrée (literally the entry) is the appetizer.

Escalope Very thin slice of meat/chicken which has been pounded so it is flat.

Glossary

Farce See **Stuffing.**

Fines herbes Chopped mixed herbs, correctly chervil, tarragon and chives, although parsley is often included.

Flamber To add flavor by pouring warmed spirits/brandy/sherry over food in a pan, igniting to burn off the alcohol and continuing to cook.

Flan Shallow pastry shell similar to a pie shell, but molded in a metal ring set on a baking sheet. Flan can also mean a baked custard.

Fold To mix a very light substance with a heavier one so as little lightness as possible is lost. Mixture must be lifted from beneath and folded over, not stirred in a circle.

Fondue Party dish usually made with Gruyère/Emmenthal cheese, white wine and/or kirsch, served at the table from a flameproof casserole over a burner. Using fondue forks, cubes of bread are dipped in. Dessert fondue is sometimes made of chocolate, and fruits and cake are used for dipping.

> **Fondue Bourguignonne.** Cubes of raw beef fillet steak are dipped into a deep pan of smoking hot oil, then into a selection of spiced sauces in separate dishes.

Fool Fruit purée mixed with thick/whipped cream.

Freeze to chill below freezing point of water. Freezers for storing food should be kept at 0°F, although refrigerator freezing compartments are often warmer.

Fricadeller Ground raw/cooked meat shaped into small balls and fried.

Fricassée 1 Reheated, cooked chicken in white sauce. **2** Stew of white meat/poultry/fish/vegetables. Usually served with a white/velouté sauce.

Fritter Cooked meat/raw or cooked vegetables/fresh fruit dipped in batter, then fried in deep fat.

Fry 1 Dry: to cook steaks/chops over high heat in fat/oil barely covering the base of a heavy frying pan. **2** Shallow: to cook eggs/fish/breaded chops briskly without burning, in $\frac{1}{4}$–$\frac{3}{4}$ inch layer of fat/oil. **3** Deep: to immerse and fry food (protected by batter/breadcrumbs/flour) in fat/oil. Most deep-fat frying is meant to seal foods and fat should be very hot. Strain used deep fat and keep, covered, for future use. Fat used for frying fish should be reserved for fish only. Drain deep-fried foods on paper towels or a wire rack.

Fumet 1 Well-reduced fish stock. **2** Essence from cooking fish/meat/game.

Garnish To decorate as you like, or to use specified garnish, e.g. ham and peppers, as with roast chicken Basquaise.

Gelatin 1 Unflavored powdered gelatin sets molds/aspics/creams; first soften in water/fruit juice, then dissolve in hot water. Gelatine is preflavored. **2** Sweet or savory mold set with powdered gelatin.

Glacé Sugar icing for cakes/cookies/candied fruits.

Glaze 1 To make shiny with egg, water and sugar, or milk. **2** Reduced bone stock or stock and gelatin glaze, used to coat cold meats. **3** Jam or fruit glaze for coating desserts and cakes.

Goulash Highly seasoned stew made with onions and (sweet) paprika.

Grate To scrape into small pieces by rubbing a hard food, like cheese/raw vegetables, on a grater.

Gratin (au) Strictly, to cook food covered in crumbs/butter/sauce/grated cheese in the oven. Term sometimes used for browning cooked food under broiler.

Grease To coat with a thin, even layer of butter/margarine/shortening.

Grind To cut food into small pieces with a grinder.

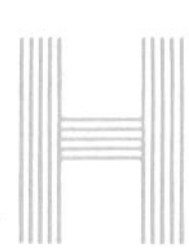

Homogenized Emulsified liquid, e.g. homogenized milk (with fat particles broken up and dispersed).

Hors d'oeuvre Hot or cold bite-sized snacks served before a meal or, especially in Europe, a first course of assorted appetizers.

Infuse To steep in warm, not necessarily boiling, liquid to draw flavor into the liquid.

Julienne 1 Fine matchstick strips of meat/vegetables usually about $\frac{1}{8}$ inch thick by $1\frac{1}{2}$–2 inches long.
2 A clear vegetable soup to which a mixture of finely shredded cooked vegetables has been added. Similar to consomme.

Knead To work a dough until smooth and elastic, preferably with the hands; especially important in bread-making.

Kneaded butter (beurre manié) See **Butter**.

Lard Rendered pork fat for frying, or used as shortening.

Lardons Small $\frac{1}{4}$ inch thick strips of fat salt pork about $1\frac{1}{2}$ inches long. Used to give extra fat to cuts of meat that have little or none of their own to protect them from drying out during cooking (see **Bard**). Strips are larded or sewn into the meat with a larding needle.

Liaison Mixture for thickening/binding sauce/gravy/soup, e.g. roux, egg yolks, cream and kneaded butter.

Macédoine Mixture of diced/sliced, cooked/raw vegetables/fruit, served hot or cold (usually with butter/dressing/mayonnaise; fruit marinated in syrup/liqueur).

Macerate To soak/infuse, usually fruit, in liqueur/syrup.

Marinade See **Marinate**.

Marinate To soak raw meat/game/fish/poultry in cooked or uncooked spiced liquid (**marinade**) of wine, oil, herbs and vegetables for hours/days before cooking. This softens, tenderizes and flavors, and a marinade can be used for making the final sauce. Use a non-porous container, such as glass/glazed enamel/stainless steel to withstand the effects of acid in wine or vinegar.

Marmelade Fruit stewed and reduced to a thick, almost solid purée or butter. Use as a pie/flan filling. Not to be confused with marmalade preserve or jam made from citrus fruits.

Meringue Light and airy mixture made of beaten egg whites and sugar.

Mirepoix Basic preparation for flavoring braises and sauces of diced vegetables, sweated (cooked gently for a few minutes in butter), to draw out flavor. Diced ham/bacon and bay leaf sometimes included.

Mousse Sweet, smooth mixture, airy but rich, made from eggs, sugar, cream with flavoring, e.g. coffee/chocolate/fruit. Savory: made from salmon/lobster/veal/chicken/cheese/vegetables, usually served chilled. Powdered gelatin may be used for setting.

Noisette 1 Small 'nut' of rolled meat without the bone, e.g. noisette of lamb. **2** Flavored with hazelnuts. **3** Nut-brown color, e.g. cook butter to a noisette.

Panada Basic thickening for fish/meat/vegetable molds made from soaked breadcrumbs, choux pastry or thick béchamel sauce.

Papillote (en) Food wrapped, cooked and served in a 'case' of oiled/buttered paper or foil. This conserves juices and aromas, especially of delicate foods, e.g. red snapper.

Parboil To boil until half-cooked, as with potatoes, before roasting.

Pare To remove a very thin layer from the surface of fruits/vegetables, with a knife/peeler.

Pasta Paste based on flour and water cut into different shapes, e.g. spaghetti, macaroni, vermicelli.

Pastry Basic mixture of flour and water, with additions of butter/margarine/shortening/milk/sugar/egg yolk/cream to produce different types of crust, e.g. pie, flaky, puff, choux.

Pâté French name for pastry. **Pâté sucrée,** a sweetened pastry, is used for flans, tartlets and pâtisserie.

Pâté Ground/pounded, cooked and well-seasoned meat/game/fish mixture, served cold, e.g. chicken liver pâté. Pâté de foie gras, made from fattened goose liver, is much richer and cooked in a terrine mold, or in pastry.

Pâtisserie Pastry/small cake.

Pectin Substance contained in some fruits and vegetables that acts as a setting agent for jams and jellies.

Pickle(s) 1 Brine used in preserving/salting meats. **2** Vegetables, e.g. onions, cucumbers, (usually first soaked in brine) preserved in spiced vinegar.

Pit To remove stones/seeds from fruit.

Pith White part of citrus fruits between peel and flesh.

Poach To cook gently in trembling (not boiling) liquid. See **Simmer.**

Pot roast To cook a cut of meat/poultry after browning in fat/oil, by simmering or steaming slowly (usually in oven) with a little liquid or in own juices in a covered casserole. The lid must be tight-fitting. Root vegetables are added for flavor. Cheaper, tougher cuts of meat benefit from slow pot roasting or braising.

Pound To reduce to a powder/smooth paste. If no mortar and pestle is available, use a heavy bowl and the end of a rolling pin.

Praline Flavoring of caramelized sugar and almonds that is used in sweet dishes.

Preserve 1 To cure/smoke/can/freeze meats/ fish/poultry/vegetables. **2** Fruit preserved with sugar to form jam/conserve.

Purée Fruit/vegetables/meat, usually pre-cooked, sieved/blended to a thick cream.

Quiche Savory custard, flavored with cheese/ ham/fish and baked in a pie shell.

Ragoût Brown stew cooked slowly without thickening.

Rare Underdone, deep pink when applied to roasted/broiled meat. See **Saignant.**

Reduce To boil down sauce/liquid to concentrate flavor and thicken the consistency.

Refresh To pour cold water over previously blanched and drained food. This 'sets' vegetable colors, cleans meat/variety meats.

Refrigerate To store food at temperatures just above freezing (around 40°F) so the bacteria that cause spoilage are relatively inactive.

Render To melt down fat gently into drippings in oven and then strain, or boil with a little water and strain when clear.

Roast to cook by direct heat, e.g. well basted with fat over an open flame or gas/electric spit. When oven roasting, meat should be set on a rack in a roasting pan with fat, and well basted during cooking.

Roux (white, blond, or brown) Fat and flour liaison mixture. This is the basis of all flour sauces (white/brown). The amount of fat added is generally about the same as that of flour. To make: melt fat, stir in flour (off heat) and pour on water/stock/milk. Then stir over heat until roux thickens, season, bring to a boil and cook as directed.

Saignant Extremely rare (applied to roasted/ broiled meat/game) so that the blood runs out when meat is cut.

Salmis Form of ragoût, usually of game/ poultry, first lightly roasted, then cut up and gently simmered for a short time in a rich, brown sauce.

Sauté To brown food in butter or oil and butter. Sometimes cooking is completed in a sauce made with food in a sauté pan.

Savory 1 Sour or salty, i.e. dish without sugar. **2** Small, piquant dish, traditionally served in Britain as the last course (to clean the palate after dessert in preparation for port), e.g. Welsh rarebit and other snacks which are served on toast. **3** An aromatic herb.

Scald 1 To plunge into boiling water for easy peeling. **2** To heat a liquid, e.g. milk, to just under boiling point.

Score To mark with a series of shallow, even cuts.

Sear To seal in valuable juices of foods, usually meat, by frying (browning) over fierce heat for a short time. Often precedes stewing/casseroling.

Seasoning Salt and pepper, also other flavorings. To 'correct' seasoning is to taste towards end of cooking process to see if more salt/pepper/other flavors are needed, and to adjust accordingly.

Shortening Fat which, when worked into flour, gives a 'short' crisp quality to pastry/ cakes. This includes lard as well as vegetable shortenings. Fats with least liquid have greatest shortening power.

Shred To cut/break into uneven strips.

Sieve To work through a sieve/food mill to obtain a purée.

Sift To shake a dry, powdered substance through a sieve/sifter to remove any lumps and give lightness.

Simmer To cook in liquid at 195°F or just below boiling point so bubbles occasionally break the surface.

Skim To remove impurities, e.g. fat/scum, from surface of sauces/soups/stocks. This is done when liquid has been slowly brought to a boil.

Soufflé Dish similar to a mousse, but of lighter consistency with beaten egg whites. It can be hot or cold, sweet or savory; traditionally should rise 1–2 inches above the rim of its straight-sided serving dish.

Souse To cover food in wine vinegar and/or wine and spices. Cook slowly and allow food to cool in the same liquid.

Spatchcock For broiling: any very small bird split down the back, flattened (skewered if necessary) and basted well with melted butter.

Steam To cook steadily in closed container (or between two plates) over a half-filled pan of steadily boiling water. Food must not touch water.

Stew 1 To cook meat/vegetables/fish/poultry slowly in liquid in a covered pan. Suited to coarse-fibered meats. **2** Brown stew: lightly brown (floured) meat in fat/oil before adding liquid. **3** White stew: put meat into cold water and bring to simmering point.

Stock Liquid made by simmering meat/bones/vegetables in liquid/water for several hours. Used for making gravy/sauce/soup. Fish stock is made by simmering fish bones with root vegetables/herbs/seasonings in water for 20 minutes.

Stuffing (dressing or **farce)** Savory ingredients, e.g. ground veal/pork, mixed with breadcrumbs/rice, vegetables, nuts, spices and often bound together with eggs/milk/sauce. Used to flavor meat/poultry/fish; stuffed into cavities or between portions; can be baked/fried separately and served with main dish.

Suet Finely ground beef fat without membrane, preferably from around kidney.

Sweat To draw out flavor by cooking diced/sliced vegetables gently in a little melted butter until soft (not browned) in a covered pan.

Syrup 1 Sugar and water boiled together to a specified temperature. Used for poaching/candying fruit, added to fresh fruit salad, etc. **2** Liquid derived from other sources of sugar, e.g. maple and corn syrup. **3 Stock syrup:** 1 cup granulated sugar dissolved in 2 cups water over gentle heat, brought to a boil and boiled for 10 minutes. Used for mixing with icing to give it a glossy appearance.

T

Tenderize To break down tough fibers in meat by heating/marinating/beating with a mallet.

Terrine 1 Seasoned meat mixture similar to that used for a pâté but usually of coarser texture. **2** Oval china/pottery mold in which the mixture is cooked.

Truss To secure legs/wings of poultry/game neatly with string/skewers to give birds a good shape and make carving easier.

Velouté One of the basic French sauces made with butter, flour and stock.

Vinaigrette A cold salad dressing made with oil and vinegar and flavored with chopped herbs.

Vol-au-vent Case of puff pastry filled with small pieces of cooked meat/poultry/shellfish in a thick sauce.

Water bath (bain marie) A large pan of simmering water, used to cook at a temperature just below boiling point. For the preparation of sauces/creams/food liable to curdle/stick to the pan if cooked over direct heat. May be done in oven or on top of stove. A double boiler gives a similar result. Sauces and other delicate dishes may be kept hot in a water bath at less than simmering heat.

Whisk To beat fast with a circular motion so that a mixture is made lighter by incorporating air. This can be done with an electric mixer on high speed/rotary beater/balloon whisk.

Glossary

CASP NETSCHER pinxt   Gem. Gallerie des Königl. Museums in Berlin.   A.H. PAYNE sc.

The Kitchen. Die Küche.

INDEX

(Volume 1)

Note: bold type indicates a color illustration

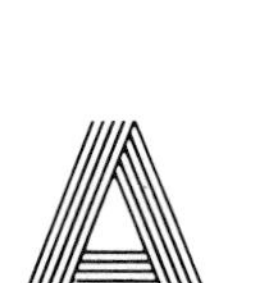

B

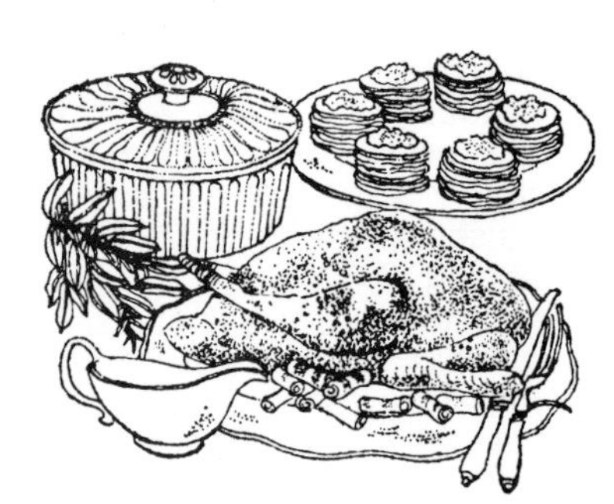

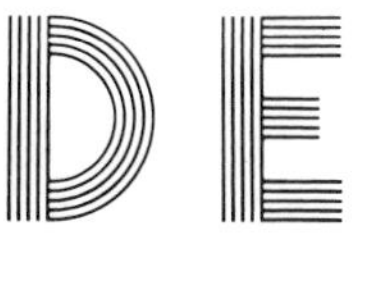

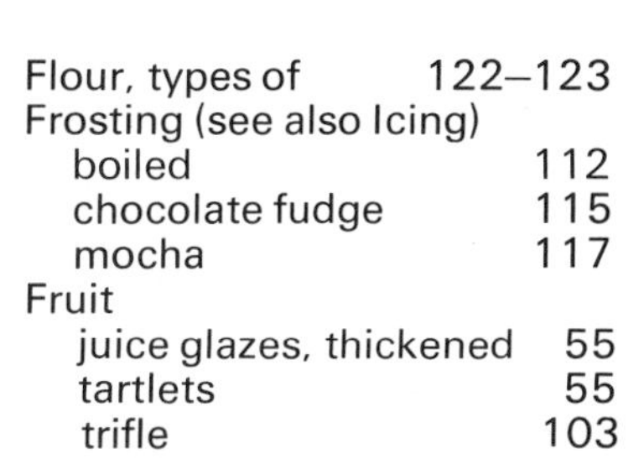

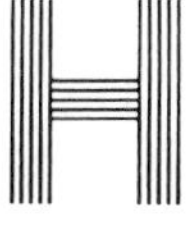

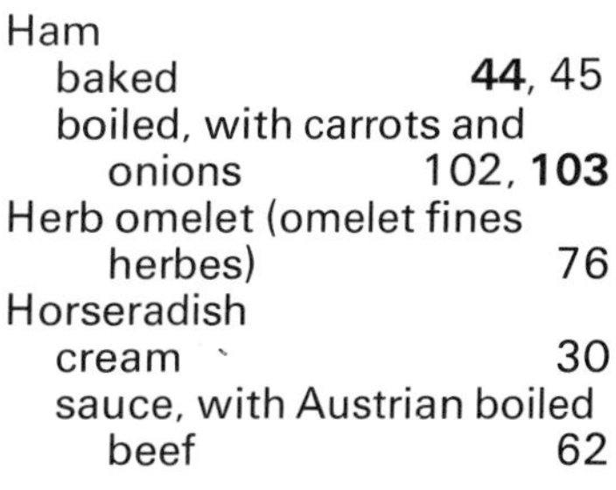

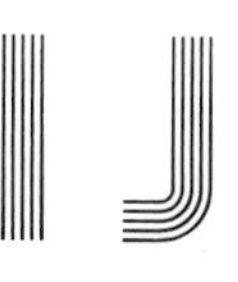

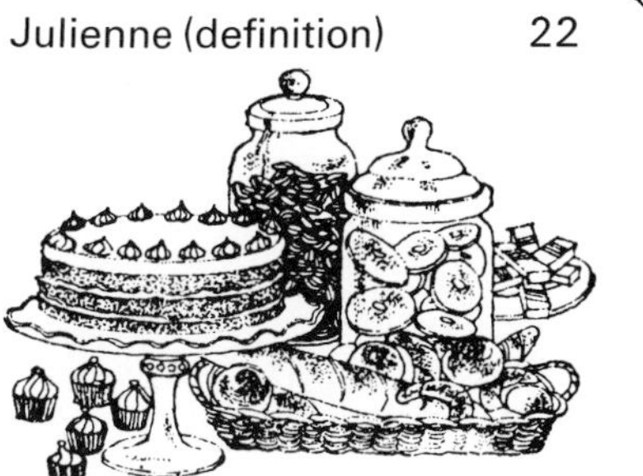

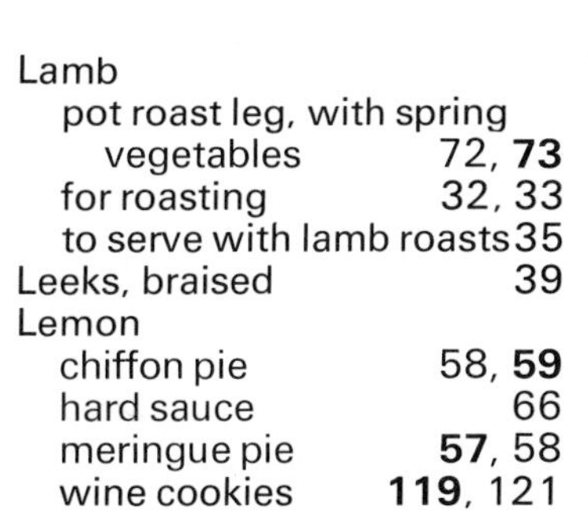

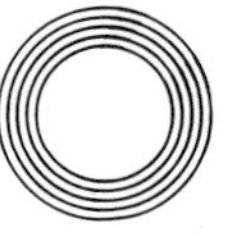

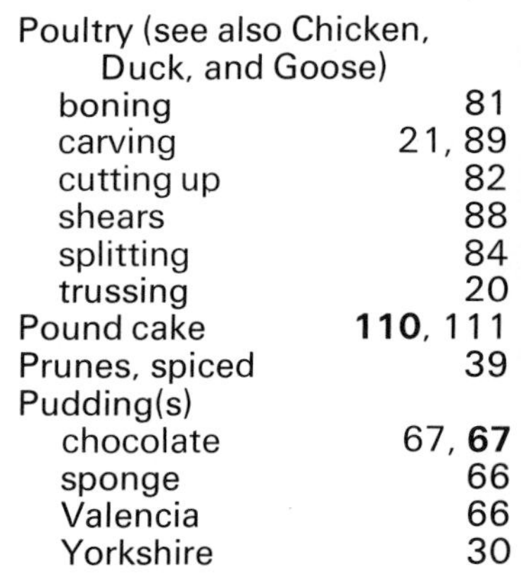

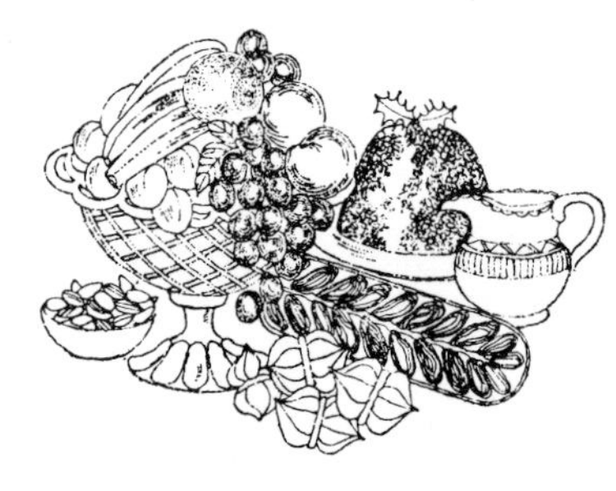

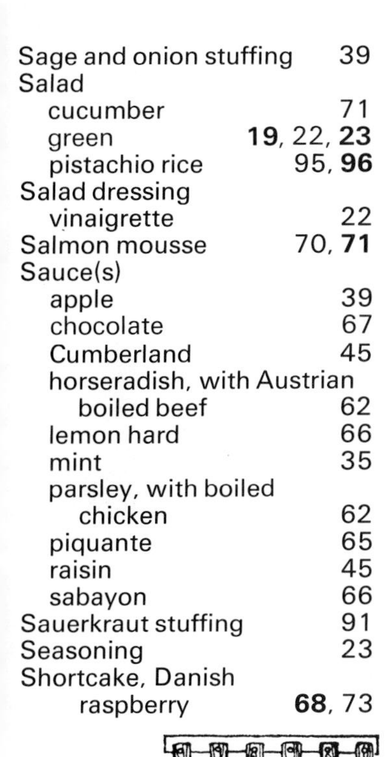

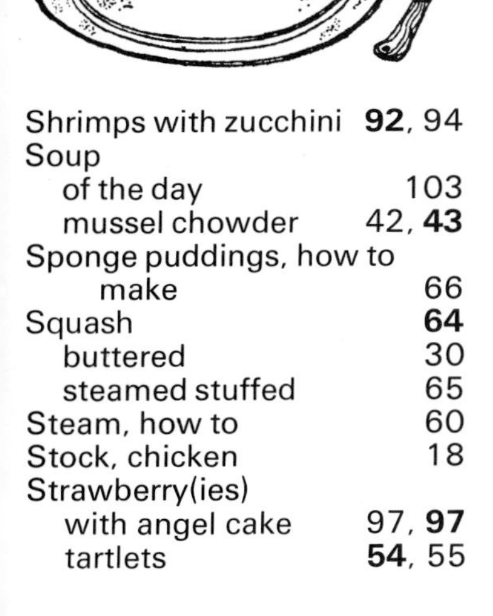

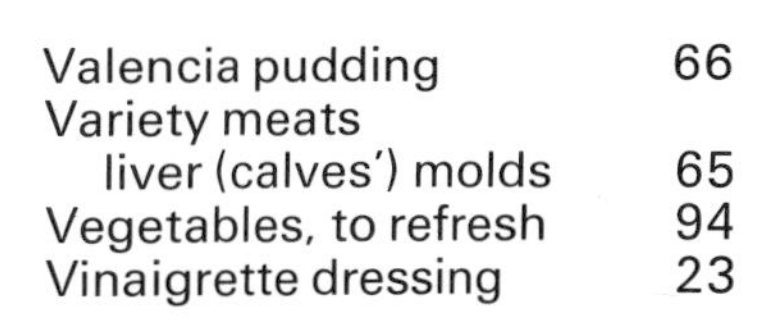

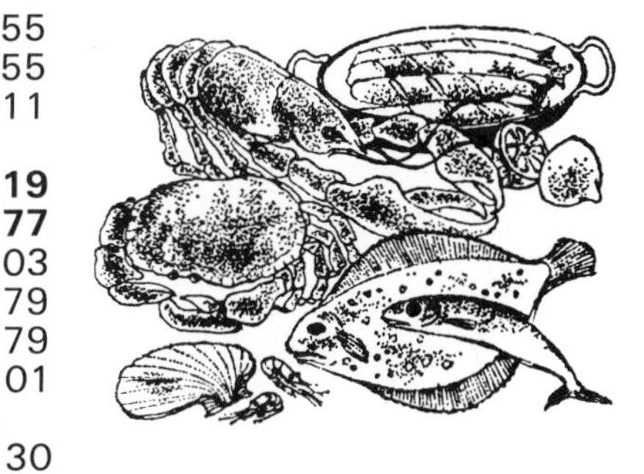

Acknowledgments

Photographs by Fred J. Maroon on pages 15, 17, 19, 23, 25, 31, 38, 43, 51, 64, 77, 87, 104 and 116. Other photographs by John Cowderoy, Michael Leale, John Ledger and Roger Phillips. Photographs on pages 2, 118–119 and illustration on page 49 courtesy of Queen Anne Press.

Notes

Notes

Notes